Totally
Pizza

SUNBELT EDITIONS
An imprint of Sunbelt Shows, Inc.
www.FieryFoodsCentral.com

© 2022 Mark Masker
All rights reserved.

Printed in the U.S.A.
Book design by Lois Manno

ISBN 978-0-9832515-8-3

Totally

Pizza

The Wild Story of the World's Most Famous Food

Mark Masker

SUNBELT
EDITIONS

Dedication

To my parents, Bill and Anne Masker. I never could have done this without their love and support.

Totally Pizza

Contents

Totally Pizza

Preface: Just Say "Dough"

Any sixth grader alive today has no idea what the world was like without computers, cell phones, or the Internet. In fact, there's a real good chance one or more of these technowonders played a part in the kid's parents hooking up in the first place. Likewise, the child's mom and dad have no idea what America was like before pizza. Chances are, neither do the grandparents, either. Although pizza has existed in one form or another for centuries, it's only been a worldwide staple for a fraction of that time.

Case in point: *I* don't know what America was like before pizza. Hell, I've been eating it as long as I've been eating solid food. Chances are, so have you. For me, the addiction started when my folks fed me the gateway drug/cardboard with tomato sauce on it that was frozen pizza in the 1970s. It was win-win for everybody. I liked it because pizza shut me up quickly when I was hungry and my folks liked it because it shut me up quickly when I was hungry.

Later on, when I was old enough to actually sit still in a restaurant seat and behave for an hour or two, I graduated to pizzeria pie like everyone else. That pretty well sealed the addiction for me. Having graduated to the higher-grade narcotic that's a good pizzeria slice, I was fully hooked.

The situation spiraled out of control in college. Left to my own devices 3500 miles from anything resembling adult supervision, I, like every other post-high school teen entering the Big Wide World, overdosed on delivery pizza every chance I could (and gained the weight to prove it). By this time, Domino's was going nationwide in the 1980s, making it super easy to get a cheap pizza fix in 30 minutes or less. Back then, I was an animation major at the University of Southern California, in Los Angeles. I didn't know it at the time, but while I was learning about drawing cartoons, Ed LaDou and Alice Waters had taken pizza out of the pizzeria and into the world of fine dining, giving birth to what we now call California-style or gourmet pizza.

Thanks to a mix of Italians migrating from Naples a hundred years ago, World War II vets scouring America for good pizza after the war, and big business bringing pizza everywhere it could, pizza has evolved from foodstuff to cultural phenom, with competitions, expos, and even one company's aerial stunt team spreading the pizza gospel all over the planet—and beyond.

Like a good pie, this book is a collection of many ingredients topping a simple base. It's also part history, part humor essay, and part freak show. You're welcome, America.

Totally Pizza

Introduction:
"Mom, Where do Pizzas Come From?"

That's a damn good question. In the broadest sense, pizza is flatbread with stuff on it. The full gamut of pizza runs from a slab of soggy cardboard topped with sausage bits (school cafeteria pizza) to flavored dough topped with goat cheese, squid ink, and puppy dog tears (gourmet pizza). Yet, the popular image of pizza is a round slab of flatbread topped with tomato sauce, mozzarella cheese, and perhaps some pepperoni. In other words, the definition of pizza is limited only by your imagination.

I like to think the reason pizza speaks to so many people around the world is because almost every culture has a history with flat bread. People tend to embrace the familiar. Giving it to them with a few changes is a lot easier than getting them to swallow a whole new animal, no matter how tasty that animal may be.

Pizza, like the wise old master in a kung fu movie, is hard to pin down. Simple in some ways, complex in others. Everyone pretty much agrees you need at least cheese, sauce, and a bread crust. What kind of cheese, what type of sauce, and how thick a crust is where you get into trouble. New Yorkers want their foldable slices, Chicagoans insist on thick pie in a deep dish, and us nutty Californians will throw anything we want on pizza and not care what you think. Naples traditionalists hate all of us for violating their darling like some slutty prom date. And that's just America's and Italy's versions!

A neon lighting sign on the wall of a Kotipizza restaurant in Ruoholahti, Helsinki, Finland.
JIP, CC BY-SA 4.0, via Wikimedia Commons

Totally Pizza

I'm not going to get into the oddball pizzas here. I have another chapter for that. Let's take a look at the basic building blocks—the DNA, if you will—of pizza: cheese, meat, sauce, and crust.

Say "Cheese!"
Cheese is probably the most varied of the three basics that comprise a pizza. The term "pizza cheese" encompasses several varieties and types of cheeses and dairy products that are designed and manufactured for use specifically on pizza, including processed and modified cheese (such as mozzarella-like processed cheeses and mozzarella variants). Mozzarella, Provolone, Cheddar and Parmesan are the most popular cheeses used on pizza. Emmental, Romano and Ricotta are often used as toppings; then, there are the other processed pizza cheeses manufactured specifically for the mass production of pizza.

That last type bears elaboration. When I say "processed cheese," I'm not talking about the liquid yellow canned substance that tastes and feels closer to plastic than actual food. Many studies and experiments have been conducted to create a pizza cheese that has the right browning, melting, stretchiness, moisture, and fat content consumers expect and love on a good pizza. Factors like vegetable oil, culture processes, and denatured whey protein are just some of the elements that've been rigorously analyzed to produce such a supercheese. Like a drug dealer doling out product on the street, it's all in how you mix—or cut—the cheese.

According to the International Dictionary of Food and Cooking, pizza cheese is "a soft spun-curd cheese similar to Mozzarella made from cow's milk" and "used particularly for pizzas and contains somewhat less water than real Mozzarella." More often than not pizza cheese blends two or more cheeses, the most common combination being low-moisture Mozzarella and Provolone.

Cheesology
No one understands how big a deal pizza cheese better than Leprino Foods Company, the world's largest manufacturer of pizza cheese. Each year, Leprino manufactures 1.2 billion pounds of the tasty stuff. They even hold a patent on a frozen shredded pizza cheese that goes from milk to finished cheese in only a few hours!

Here in the U. S., some cheeses are more popular in some regions than others. Whole milk mozzarella is the cheese of choice in the East and Southwest. Cheddar shines in the Southeast, while Provolone is popular on both coasts. Provel cheese is the name of the game in St. Louis, where it was developed specifically for that type of cracker-like pizza.

Totally Pizza

Ever take a close look at the cheese on a frozen pizza? Did you notice how the cheese looks a lot different than grated pizza cheese in the dairy aisle? That's not just the freezing process. Sometimes the cheese on frozen pie is granulated.

Quiz

True or False: Some estimates state that only 40% of all pizza cheese in the United States is actual mozzarella cheese.
Correct Answer: False. The estimates are even lower than that. Try 30%.

In 1997 it was estimated that 2 billion pounds of pizza cheese a year was produced in the United States. How much pizza cheese was produced in Europe?
A. 100 million pounds
B. 200 million pounds
C. 300 million pounds
D. 50 million pounds
Correct Answer: B. 200 million pounds

Those Cheesy Water Buffaloes

No, you're not missing something. *Mozzarella di bufala* is, in fact, Italian for "buffalo mozzarella." That's because in Naples, they make their Mozzarella from the milk of domestic water buffalo.

Production of real *Mozzarella di Bufala Campana* isn't just limited to one part of Italy, though. You'll find it being made from Rome to Salerno. It's a $430 million a year industry in Italy, with 16 percent of the 33,000 tons being exported mostly to France and Germany, but it's starting to catch on in Russia and Japan, too. Other countries all over the world make it, from the U. S. to Thailand, Argentina to Australia.

As for how the water buffalo got to Italy in the first place, that's a really good question. One story says Goths brought Asian water buffaloes to Italy during raids and conquests, er, I mean, migrations, in the Middle Ages. Another source agrees with the medieval part but credits Normans from Sicily circa 1000 AD. The Consorzio per la Tutela also refers to fossil evidence suggesting that water buffalo may have originated in Italy. It's also possible that Arabs brought them to the Near East out of Mesopotamia, and that European crusaders brought the animals home with them as spoils. Big, bad- tempered spoils that apparently produce yummy cheese.

Feelin' Saucy

Tomato sauce is the mortar that unites any pizza, but gen-you-wine Neapolitan-style pizza sauce is marinara, or "mariner's" sauce. It's a southern Italian sauce comprised of tomatoes, herbs, garlic, and onions. People sometimes tweak it with olives, capers, and other spices, but it doesn't have nearly the variation as pizza cheese.

No one knows who really came up with marinara sauce. I suppose we could hold a séance in Naples and use the blood of innocents to attract the long-dead spirit of a 16th century pizzaiolo and ask him, but that's a lot of work.

There are at least two theories about how humanity came to be blessed with marinara's presence. One says Neapolitan sailors' wives used to serve it to their hubbies upon their return from sea voyages. The second tells us cooks on Neapolitan ships invented it in the 1550s after the tomato came back to Spain from the Americas. The high acidity of tomatoes made the sauce great for long sea voyages, since it was resistant to spoiling. That's a huge plus when the nearest refrigerator is three or four centuries away.

The first hard evidence for marinara's age comes from Italian chef Antonio Latini, who served as the Steward of the First Minister to the Spanish Viceroy of Naples in the 17th century. His cookbook, *Lo Scalo alla Moderna* (aka. *The Modern Steward*), makes the first written mention of tomato sauce. It was published in two volumes in 1692 and 1694.

Be Careful What You Ask For
Ordering marinara sauce in some parts of the world can be quite exciting—especially if you have a seafood allergy. Outside of Naples and the United States, "marinara" often refers to a sauce containing seafood. "Marinara" being Italian for "marine," you can see why that might be.

San Marzanos: The Champagne of Tomatoes
Many chefs consider San Marzano tomatoes to be the best paste tomatoes in the world, and no pizza would be the real deal to a Neapolitan without them. This plum tomato is thinner than a Roma, and has a more pointed end. It has a stronger, sweeter flavor, is less acidic, and has fewer seeds, too.

When canneries started using San Marzanos commercially in 1926, the chefs loved them. In Italy, canned San Marzanos grown in the Valle del Sarno, may be classified as Pomodoro S. Marzano dell'Agro Sarnese-Nocerino and have Europe's DOP endorsement. DOP is a mercifully short way of saying "Denominazione d' Origine Protetta" (or "protected designation of origin" in English). It's similar to the way all champagnes are sparkling wines, but a sparkling wine isn't champagne unless it's from Champagne in France. San Marzano also refers to the region of Italy where the tomatoes come from. San Marzanos can be (and are) grown elsewhere, but they don't get the real deal label.

Totally Pizza

These tomatoes don't come cheap, either. That's why Italy has a counterfeit tomato problem. In 2010, Italy's carabinieri confiscated 1,470 tons of canned tomatoes with erroneous labels on them. San Marzano tomatoes also the only acceptable tomatoes for making Vera Pizza Napoletana (True Neapolitan Pizza) to AVPN standards. (More on the AVPN in Chapter 2.)

The story goes that the seeds for the San Marzano were gifted to the Kingdom of Naples by the Viceroyalty of Peru back in 1770. Whether or not that's the case, San Marzanos come from the town of the same name near Naples and were first grown in the nutrient-rich volcanic soil at the foot of Mount Vesuvius.

Pepperoni

Ah, pepperoni. That most traditional of pizza meats, with its distinct molten reddish grease and little spicy kick. Oh, how I love you. I just wish you'd drop the act and stop letting everyone think you come from Italy.

Seriously, though, pepperoni is about as Italian as Olive Garden's breadsticks. Don't get me wrong, I love them both. Neither one really comes from the Old Country, though. The truth is, pepperoni was most likely invented by Italian immigrants in the United States. The earliest written reference to it I've seen comes from the Northeast in 1919.

"This pie's okay but it needs little sausage wafers." A 1950's-era pizza pie platter. Public Domain image

Totally Pizza

Even the name isn't truly Italian. Like the meat itself, the word *pepperoni* is the mutant American cousin of another one: *peperone*, the Italian word for bell pepper and its relatives. As for pepperoni the sausage, it's an offshoot of Italian salami. More specifically, pepperoni is cousin to the spiced salamis of south Italy like *salsiccia Napoletana piccante*. What separates them are pepperoni's finer grain, softer consistency, and the fact that it's not aged as long.

Most of the time pepperoni is made from cured beef or pork, with peppers, garlic, mustard seed, or fennel bringing different levels of spice and variations in flavor. None of which makes pepperoni pink and orange. For that you can thank sodium nitrite and paprika, respectively.

Part I

Pizza in Italy

Pizzeria Brandi in Naples, Italy. This was the birthplace of Margherita Pizza in 1889. Public domain image

The Italian Job

"...a species of most nauseating cake... covered over with slices of pomodoro or tomatoes, and sprinkled with little fish and black pepper and I know not what other ingredients, it altogether looks like a piece of bread that had been taken reeking out of the sewer." —Samuel Morse, c. 1831

That review doesn't exactly glow, does it? Yet, that's exactly how non-Neapolitans viewed modern pizza in its infancy—the key word here being "modern." If you want to know when pizza really originated, the question is, "How far back do you want to go?" The Byzantine empire? The Roman empire? The ancient Greeks? The word "pizza" probably first came into use in 997 AD. Pizza as a concept, however, predates that by centuries. Unless you have a time machine, you'll never really know who created the very first pizza. If you do have a time machine, you have better things to do than watch some cave man make bread. Some claim that pizza has been in Italy since the dawn of upright stance. They say that the first "pizza" was a crude bread that was baked under the hot stones of a clan's cook fire. With the discovery of seasonings, prehistoric foodies jazzed the bread up. The bread also multi-tasked as a plate for soaking up all that extra sabertooth tiger gravy.

Here's one of the earliest recorded references to a diner using a flatbread plate that does double duty as part of the meal:

"Beneath a shady tree, the hero spread
His table on the turf, with cakes of bread;
And, with his chiefs, on forest fruits he fed.
They sate; and, (not without the god's command,)
Their homely fare dispatch'd, the hungry band
Invade their trenchers next, and soon devour,

3

Totally Pizza

To mend the scanty meal, their cakes of flour.
Ascanius this observ'd, and smiling said:
"See, we devour the plates on which we fed."
—The Aeneid, by Virgil, c. 19 BC

Marcus Gavius Apicius was a semi-mythical gourmet who lived in Campania during the first century AD. We get a lot of our insights into ancient Roman cooking from his writings, which cover such weird topics as how delicious flamingo tongue tastes. Allegedly, he was such a hardcore foodie that when his finances dried up, he poisoned himself to avoid dying of hunger. People mistakenly refer to *De Re Coquinaria* as one of his works because of its other name, *Apicius*. The book he *didn't* write has recipes for stuffing hollowed out bread with different ingredients, including those used in pizza, like a proto-calzone.

Think about it—pizza is flatbread with tasty stuff on it. There isn't a culture in the Mediterranean that doesn't make some variation on this basic theme. And these cultures just loved to conquer each other, so they talked, and shared...sometimes, even willingly. The Romans were especially fond of conquest as a pastime. Chevy didn't make a Corvette back then, so Roman leaders had to deal with their midlife crises by conquering people, enslaving them, and bringing them home to show off at parties. Romans also incorporated these cultures into their own, especially that of the Greeks, whose flatbread fare made an indelible mark on the Italian peninsula.

Four centuries after Julius Caesar took power, the Roman Empire had some serious issues, in the form of barbarian invasions from Gaul and Germania. As my Roman civics professor told us in college, "The Roman Empire didn't die. It moved." Where, you ask? East, to Byzantium, also known as Constantinople. Although now it's Istanbul, not Constantinople (the joke was there, I couldn't resist). In 540 AD, Emperor Justinian thought it would be a great idea to get the band back together, so he sent General Belisarius to Europe with an army and a mandate. Like the conquered Greeks that came before, these conquer-

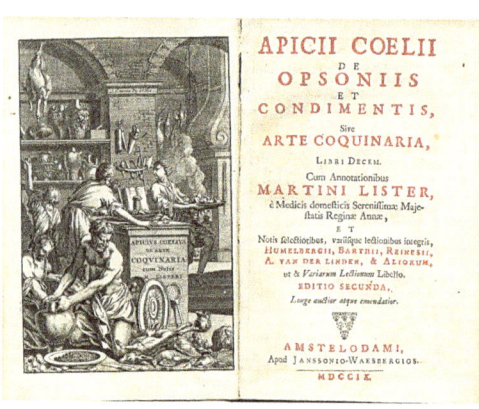

The early cookbook *De Re Coquinaria*, also known as *Apicius*. Public Domain image

4

Totally Pizza

ing Greeks brought flatbread with them for the trip. Only this time, it was what we know today as pita bread. Belisarius, who was one of the studliest generals in history, managed to reunite much of the old empire under Justinian's rule, despite his paranoid boss repeatedly tying the General's hands behind his back and not giving him enough backup to really seal the deal. He was ultimately forced to go back home, but the bread stayed behind.

Dough versus the Volcano

The year 79 AD was probably as good a time as any to be in Pompeii, right up until August 24, when Mount Vesuvius went all *Raiders of the Lost Ark* and fried or melted everybody like a bunch of Nazis looking into the wrong box. It was bad news for the locals at the time, but great for archaeologists of the future. Among the preserved artifacts trapped in time by the blast were baked flat flour cakes eaten there and in a nearby town called Naples. Some of the Pompeii shops had marble slabs and other tools similar to what you'd find in a pizzeria. Utensils weren't the only things preserved by the Vesuvius eruption. Sadly, the local people were encased in ash where they stood. One of these poor unfortunate people resides at the Museo Nazionale at Naples. Because of its stance, it bears the name *Il pizzaiolo* (the pizza maker).

In a twist of irony that would not be lost on the now-statuary inhabitants of old Pompeii, Mount Vesuvius' rich volcanic soil gives Campania's San Marzano tomatoes the qualities that many chefs say make them the best sauce tomatoes on the planet. Some people have even likened their flavor to bittersweet chocolate. They're longer than Roma tomatoes, have a thicker flesh, and a stronger taste.

Legend has it that the first San Marzanos were a present from Peru to the King of Naples in 1770, who had them planted

An ancient pizza oven from Pompeii. Photo by Deror_avi via Wikimedia Commons

Totally Pizza

near Mount Vesuvius. Because of their association with the city of Naples, San Marzano tomatoes are the official tomatoes of true Neapolitan pizza.

Frankenpizza Leaves the *Laboratoro*

In 997 AD, the word "pizza" came into use but it was another six hundred years before the basic "modern" pizza was born in Naples in the sixteenth century. It was a food for the poor and got about as much respect—as demonstrated by Mr. Morse's quote, above. At first, pizza makers seemed to place the emphasis on "cheap" rather than "tasty". Early pizza was topped with salt, lard, garlic, and sometimes pepper. *Pizzaiolos* (the official name for pizza chefs) spent long hours making the pizzas, then took them out on the street on a cart, with an oiled board for slicing them up to order. Some also sold pizza directly from their bakeries. Those first *pizzaioli* worked out of hole-in-the-wall outlets called, of all things *laboratori*.

Since pizza was a food for the slightly underfunded hoi polloi of Naples, the policy of *pizza a otto* was developed. The basic idea was that customers with no money could eat now and pay within eight days. Needless to say, if you died in that time, you didn't have to pay. It was an early reverse layaway plan, along the lines of what was practiced by Popeye's friend Wimpy when he said, "I'll gladly pay you Tuesday for a hamburger today."

Right about that time a little thing called the Age of Discovery was changing the world forever, including pizza. European explorers, looking for a faster route to India and China so they could make a fortune in tea and spices, accidentally bumped into the Americas instead. They set up shop, trading religious persecution, small pox, syphilis, and alcoholism for gold, silver, sugar, cocoa, tobacco, and precious stones. Somewhere in this economic maelstrom, tomatoes made their way

While tomatoes were considered to be deadly poison, lighting up a cancer stick and smoking your brains out was considered healthy and good for you. Well played, tobacco importing bastards. Well played. Smoking Club by James Gilvray, 1793 etching. Courtesy of ushistory.org

6

to Spain and Italy, possibly as early as 1493. They weren't immediately considered a food, however. Europeans were a tad gun shy about munching on them, since other fruits in the nightshade family had done them wrong in the past. In fact, tomatoes were thought to be poisonous.

Eventually, some impoverished and/or curious soul was desperate enough to bite into the "poisonous" fruit. Can you imagine the pleasant surprise of being the first European to bite into a tomato, only to discover its wonderful taste, followed by the even more pleasant surprise of not falling to the ground and convulsing to death? By the 17th century, *pizzaiolos* were using it as a topping on their product, and "modern" pizza was born.

Obviously, this wasn't the last pizza innovation. Antica Pizzeria Port'Alba is widely accepted as the first known pizzeria in the world. The Naples operation started as a stand in 1738, but by 1830, it was a full-on pizzeria, with seating for customers. Making the leap from street stand to full-blown restaurant was a big step taken by many of the Naples pizzerias, giving us the stereotypical pizza joints we've all come to know and love. Some of those early pizzerias are still operating today! I wonder how many McDonald's restaurants will still be operating two centuries from now?

These are just a few of the earliest pizzerias in Naples, some of which are still in business to this day.
Zi' Ciccio (1727)
Ntuono (1732)
Antica Pizzeria Port'Alba (1738)
Capasso (1750)
Da Pietro (1760) Later became Antica Pizzeria Brandi

Pizza-slumming with the Royals

One of these venerable establishments is Pizzeria Brandi, whose legendary status was officially secured in 1889. As the story goes, Italy's Queen Margherita and her hubby King Umberto I of Savoy were touring Italy, and by the time they hit Naples, they were sick to death of the French cuisine that was so *en vogue* at the time. Their royal minions summoned Pizzaiolo Raffaele Esposito of Pizzeria di Pietro e Basta Cosi (later renamed Pizzeria Brandi), and tasked him to create three different pizzas for the royal palate. The Queen favored the one topped with mozzarella, tomatoes, and basil, representing the three colors of the Italian flag. That pizza bears her name to this day, and Pizzeria Brandi still has the thank-you note from her staff displayed on its wall.

Totally Pizza

King Ferdinand IV and Queen Margherita of Savoy.
Public Domain images via Wikimedia Commons

You'd think after Pizza Margherita received its celebrity endorsement, pizza would have lived happily ever after, its place secure in Italian history. Nope—Queen Margherita apparently didn't have the same street creds as Paris Hilton or Lady Gaga—pizza remained a lowly, regional food in Italy until after World War II.

Margherita was not the only Italian noble to be smitten by a love of pizza. King Ferdinand IV of Naples was trained from a young age to be a Jedi Master of ineffectiveness. His power-grubbing regent, Bernardo Tanucci, raised the prince-who-would-be-king on a robust diet of overindulgence and idle entertainment, including slumming it with Naples' lowest class, the *lazzaroni*. That may be where Ferdinand picked up his love for pizza. When you lie with dogs, you get fleas. When you lie with poor folks in Naples, apparently you get pizza. During his reign (1751-1825), he had a pizza oven built at his summer palace. Some people say Ferdinand did this because his wife, Maria Carolina (sister of Marie Antoinette), the hardass behind the throne, wouldn't allow pizza in the main palace. Other versions of the tale say she was the one with the pizza fetish. Either way, he was still a lazy bastard.

Buffalo Soldiers

True or False: The *Consorzio per la Tutela del Formaggio di Bufala Campana* (in English, "The Consortium for the Protection of the Buffalo Cheese of Campania") is an

Totally Pizza

organization that acts as Mozzarella di Bufala Campana's personal Justice League and is responsible for "the protection, surveillance, promotion, and marketing" of the stuff.

Correct Answer: Absolutely true. Totally over the top and insecure, but true.

Quiz

True or False: The 200th anniversary of the first use of *mozzarella di bufala* was celebrated in 1976 as The Bisontennial.

False, of course. *Mozzarella di bufala,* which is considered one of the hallmarks of a classic Neapolitan pizza, has its origins shrouded in history. No one knows for sure when domesticated water buffalo were introduced to Italy. Some sources hold the Goths responsible, saying they brought the animals over from Asia in the Middle Ages. The concisely-named Consorzio per la Tutela del Formaggio Mozzarella di Bufala Campana tells us that the Normans may have introduced them to Italy in 1000 AD, or that fossilized remains suggest the animals were in Italy all along. Anyway, what's really important is that you now have the word "Bisontennial" permanently etched into your brain. No need to thank me.

But seriously, folks: Hitler wasn't exactly the poster child for a lot of things, like good sportsmanship or proper impulse control. Production of *mozzarella di bufala* ceased in World War II when his retreating troops slaughtered the Naples water buffalo herds. Production resumed soon after the war ended, though. You can't keep a good water buffalo down. No, seriously. They weigh a shitload and have a nasty temper. If a water buffalo wants to get up, you'd best let him.

Here's a breakdown of the steps needed to make *Mozzarella di Bufala Campana.*

• Milk water buffalo. Avoid the ones that have only one "udder."

• Raw buffalo milk is then stored in big steel containers

• The milk is heated and

Water Buffalo at lunch: The real fun is watching them try to pull their heads out afterward. Photo by Bobscola, CC BY-SA 4.0, via Wikimedia Commons

poured into a cream separator
- Natural whey is introduced for curdling
- The curd lies in tubs until it matures and reaches a pH value of 4.95 or so
- It's then spun with hot water poured into the curd to soften it up
- Special rotating machines shape it
- The cheese is immersed in cold water to cool
- Pickling in tubs containing the original whey
- Finally, it's packaged in special film or in basins and plastic

Various Vintage Pizza Quotes

"The pizza is a kind of which is made in St. Denis; it is round in shape and made with bread dough. At first it looks like a simple food, but examined more closely, it seems complicated." —nineteenth-century French Author Alexandre Dumas

"The blackened aspect of the toasted crust, the whitish sheen of garlic and anchovy, the greenish-yellow tint of the oil and fried herbs, and the bits of red from the tomato here and there give pizza the appearance of complicated filth that matches the dirt

Infamous pizza-hater Carlo Collodi/Lorenzi, author of *The Adventures of Pinocchio*. Public Domain image via Wikimedia Commons

of the vendor." —Italian author Carlo Collodi/Lorenzini (author of *The Adventures of Pinocchio*)

"'Pizza' may be seen in every street in Naples. It is a kind of biscuit, crisp and flavored with cheese, recognisable at a glance by the little fish, like whitebait, which are embedded in its brown surface, dusted over with green chopped herbs. I cannot recommend the dainty from personal knowledge, but Neapolitan tradition is strongly in its favor." —From *Naples: Past and Present* by Arthur Hamilton Norway, 1905, page 128.

"The famous *pizzerie* of Naples, some of which boast a hundred years of existence, are devoted exclusively

Totally Pizza

to the manufacture and sale of a sort of rustic pie, or short-cake made out of risen dough, sharply beaten till quite thin, and seasoned on top with a great deal of lard, tomatoes, and grated cheese, or, on fast-days, with olive-oil, fresh anchovies, and a touch of garlic. The brisk tapping and slapping of the *pizze* can be heard a block away, and is as characteristic as the sonorous call of the sellers: 'Have some breakfast! Have some breakfast!' You can buy a slice on the street from one of the runners, or, if you prefer, can enter the shop, stand by while your pizza is being vigorously thumped and slapped, can see it cooked in the glowing oven under the fierce heat of a lateral fire of wood shavings, whisked out on an iron shovel in three minutes' time, and served to you in popular style on a tin plate, all for three cents." —"Breakfast in Naples" by Mary Scott-Uda from *The Century* Magazine, Vol. 62, pp. 19-20 May, 1901.

Hail to the Chef

George Washington never slept there, but Di Matteo is a Naples pizzeria with the distinction of serving President Clinton when he stopped by during the G7 summit. Mention him, and they'll offer you a souvenir fake passport with his picture in it. Il Pizzaiolo del Presidente is another Naples pizzeria pimping Clinton's visit. Unlike Di Matteo, this place also claims that its grotto housed resistance fighters during World War II.

Pizza Margherita at Di Matteo, Naples. Photo by Richard Mortel. https://www.flickr.com/photos/prof_richard/48749694492

Dough Nuts and Pizza Pride

"Fortunately the Italian people has not yet accustomed itself to eat many times a day, and possessing a modest level of living, it feels deficiency and suffering less."—As quoted in *Garlic and Oil: Food and Politics in Italy* (2006) by Carol F. Helstosky

As fascist dictators go, I think of Benito Mussolini as the bad soap opera girlfriend torn between two alpha males. At first he started off on the left in the camp of commie bad boy Joe Stalin, but later on that naughty Hitler over on the right grew on Benito. He left his beau Joe once the shine wore off the red star. Then, like any good drama queen, Ben had a tumultuous affair with his new partner all over Europe. It all came to an abrupt end when the Allies laid down the law. That said, if I ever write and sell a Hollywood biopic about Mussolini, I think it would be the perfect role for Susan Lucci.

Italy's populace, much like the family members of a bad soap opera girlfriend, grew tired of Benito's character after World War II ended. They cancelled his program with two lead slugs in his chest in 1945, then proceeded to prove the above quote wrong by rebuilding the country and expressing their national pride with their cuisine, particularly pizza and pasta.

Up until the Second World War, pizza hadn't been recognized as a

Caricature of Mussolini getting kicked in the ass. Arthur Szyk, Public domain, via Wikimedia Commons

13

national food in Italy. Although Neapolitans in the 1890s were sick of the whole poverty business and many bailed for greener pastures in northern Italy or North America, pizza was still an "our" thing in Naples and not an "all of us Italians" thing.

The European reconstruction and America's rise as a dominant world power changed all of that. While everybody cleaned up the mess made by the Axis' little tryst in Europe, some Italians relocated to neighboring countries, bringing Italian food staples—like pizza—with them. By the 1960s, pizzerias were showing up in places like Scandinavia, and even in Japan.

American troops did their part too. When they weren't on duty, they spent some of their free time soaking in local culture like an army of accidental tourists (pun intended). Their desire for pizza in all parts of Italy, coupled with increased tourism in the decades following the war, brought pizza into the national spotlight in Italy. Today, Italians eat more than 2.5 billion pizza slices a year, and there are over 38,000 pizzerias in Italy.

By the 1970s pizza was hugely popular—not only in Italy but all over the States, as well. While Italians took pride in the role traditional pizza played in defining their national identity (especially in Naples), Americans were busy either homogenizing it or tweaking it with all kinds of toppings not found anywhere near Naples. Many com-

Pizzaiolos in training at the AVPN.
Photo courtesy of the Associazione Verace Pizza Napoletana

Totally Pizza

panies and pizza businesses outside of Italy advertised these variants as "Original Neapolitan Pizza," which it totally wasn't. Some Italians took umbrage to that, and a lot of old school *pizzaiolos* were downright pissed off. Come the 1980s, a far more implacable brand of dictator arose in Italy than Mussolini could ever have hoped to become...The Pizza Geek.

The Birth of Pizza Purity

Okay, "dictator" may be a tad strong. Having written for several custom Harley-Davidson magazines over the last twelve years, and being a serious comic book/sci fi/fantasy nerd to boot, I've developed a pet theory: the only thing separating hardcore Harley geeks from basement-dwelling comic book nerds is the winged logo. Here's another way of looking at it—someone who picks up a stray puppy and buys it a dog bed is an enthusiast. Someone who cups a dog's package at the Westminster Dog Show every year is a dog geek. No matter what the subject, there will always be the purists, those zealots whose lives are dedicated to a hobby, sports team, food, you name it.

In 1984, Antonio Pace founded the *Associazione Verace Pizza Napoletana* (AVPN) to preserve true Neapolitan pizza. The organization trains and certifies chefs in the production of Neapolitan-style pizza. In one sense, these folks are defenders of modern pizza's origins, educating interested pizza makers in the elements of classic Neapolitan style. In another, they're true zealots. The AVPN has rules not only for what constitutes authentic Neapolitan pizza, but also things like allowable technique and approved ingredient suppliers. They offer a 50-hour course in Naples pizza-making that lasts six days, and you can only take the training in Naples itself. Upon successful completion, you get a certificate identifying you as a "gen-you-wine" Naples *pizzaiolo*. Just don't let it go to your head.

AVPN came to be when Antonio Pace and others felt that standardized, "corporate" pizza was diverting world attention from pizza's true heritage in much the same way some Star Trek purists felt the Next Generation eclipsed and/or contradicted the original series, or classic rock lovers felt that big business slew the soul of rock music in the 1980s and 1990s. Of course, if you've ever seen the regulations for some of the traditional food organizations in other countries, you know that Europeans don't exactly have a monopoly on rules governing cooking. Yeah, that's right. I'm looking at you, Kansas City Barbecue Society competitions and International Chili Society cookoffs.

Come July 1, 1997, the AVPN and the mayor of Naples took the case for VPN (Verace Pizza Napoletana) to the Trademarks and Patents Office of the Chamber

Totally Pizza

of Commerce in Rome. They brought with them a 30-page Protocol detailing their pizza rules, as laid down by the AVPN, Professor Carlo Mangoni and the *pizzaiolos* in 1984. The goal here was DOC—*Denominazione di origine controllata.* In English, that's "Controlled Designation of Origin." All kinds of traditional European foods and beverages have DOC or similar stamps that designate what does—or does not—make something the real deal. Basically, if it isn't produced using prescribed methods and ingredients, possibly in a prescribed region, "it" isn't official. Remember that bottle of champagne you cracked open for New Year's? Unless it was made in the Champagne region of France, what you were drinking was technically sparkling wine, not champagne. The same applies here—it isn't true Neapolitan pizza unless you have the official seal-of-approval. Apparently, Europeans don't like their cuisine served in cardboard boxes, as they're not acceptable for Neapolitan pizza (or for champagne, for that matter). In 2009, things got even more official when the EU made Pizza Napoletana a Guaranteed Traditional Specialty, protecting it as such under the law.

"We are fighting nobody, we just want to affirm our ancient traditions. We are against the cultural and commercial deformation of our pizza and against its industrialization; in fact, the ready-to-eat and frozen pizzas sold in supermarkets have nothing to do with the original ones."—Antonio Pace of AVPN

The Pizza House Rules
If you want your pizza to be considered *Vera Pizza Napoletana* (aka True Neapolitan Pizza) by AVPN standards, it has to be made by the following rules:
The pizza can only be made using flour, natural yeast, or brewer's yeast, salted to taste, with water as needed. You can't use fat of any kind in the dough.
Pizza diameter cannot exceed 10-12 inches (30 cm).
AVPN rules recognize only the following as true Neapolitan pizzas:
   Marinara: tomato, oregano, garlic, olive oil, and salt.
   Margherita: tomato, mozzarella, olive oil, basil, and salt
   Al Formaggio: grated Parmigiano, lard, garlic, basil, salt. You can use tomato as an optional ingredient.
   Calzone: The dough may be stuffed with salami, ricotta, olive oil, and salt.
The AVPN website says variations on the above are allowed, provided they don't violate the rules of good taste and culinary laws. Now that leaves some latitude, especially in the Southern U.S. ...deep-fried butter-stuffed pizza, anyone?
The dough has to be kneaded by hand or by approved mixers that don't overheat the

dough. Overheating accelerates fermentation, which is great for that bathtub hooch you're making, not so much for pizza dough.

The dough must be punched down by hand. Period. You're not even allowed to use a rolling pin. FYI to any serial killers in the audience—you cannot use a severed hand as a rolling pin to get around this rule. And please, please, please, don't blame me for that.

Your oven must be made of *materiale refrattario* (refractory material similar to volcanic stone) and brick. It must also be wood-fired. So toss all those coal-fired pizzas into the garbage, New Yorkers.

Cooking takes place directly on the floor of the oven, without the use of pans, foil, or containers of any kind.

Proper oven temperature is 750-800 degrees F. (400 degrees Centigrade).

Quiz

Question: Which of these is not part of the AVPN master *pizzaiolo* course curriculum:

(A) 4 hours of theory

(B) 28 hours of laboratory practice

(C) 16 hours of professional practice

(D) 2 hours of delivery driver training on the streets of Naples

Answer: (D)

Delivering true Pizza Napoletana is a no-no. It may only be served in-house. All of the other choices really are part of the rigorous six-day pizza boot camp that is the master *pizzaiolo* certification course. If you do end up taking it, you'll shell out 2,000 Euros for the training cost alone.

The World Pizza Championship and Other Sporting Events

Competitive spectacle has been a part of Italy (and Western culture) ever since the first lion in a Roman arena chowed down on its first Christian. Italian culture has come a long way since then, and sports have become decidedly less one-sided. The World Pizza Championship takes place every year and is a throw down to determine the world's best pizza makers. It started in 1991 and is organized by the magazine *Pizza e Pasta Italiana* and *PizzaNew*. Nowadays, over 20 countries compete every year, and in 2012, over 500 pizza chefs were expected to show up. Pizzas are judged by preparation, taste, and presentation.

Competing isn't limited to just making pizza, though. Other contests include fastest pizza maker, freestyle acrobatics, and the largest dough stretch. The World Pizza

Totally Pizza

Pizza spinning is universal to the making of pizza, and is a popular competitive sport among *pizzialos.* Jeff Kubina from Columbia, MD, CC BY-SA 2.0 via Wikimedia Commons

Championship calls Salsomaggiore Terme (Parma), Italy home. Each year Miss Italy acts as the official hostess and crowns the winners. Other European cities have big pizza games too, including Naples and Paris.

Italians have a reputation for their pizza that rivals their passion for soccer. Both of these worlds collided during the `06 World Cup semi-finals when Italy faced off against Germany. German news media fanned the flames, talking all kinds of mad smack about the Italians, calling them "pizza-eating mama's boys," and in some cases even urging Germans to order a ton of pizza during the game in order to keep Italians too busy working in their pizzerias to cheer for their countrymen. As an alternative, German fans were encouraged to boycott the food altogether. The Italian team repaid Germany for the insult in the only currency that really mattered—the Italians won.

Roman Pizza vs. Naples Pizza vs Sicilian Pizza vs. Godzilla vs Dracula vs. Billy the Kid

I'd see a movie about three giant pizzas fighting those other three characters, for the

Totally Pizza

cheesiness if nothing else (tap tap tap; is this microphone on?). All semi-kidding aside, Neapolitan pizza is almost as different from its Roman and Sicilian kin as it is from that America. When a Neapolitan *pizzaiolo* whips it out, the first thing American tourists notice is just how much smaller it is than what they've seen back home. We are of course talking about pizza, not "sausage." Unlike the huge sliced pizzas you get from Domino's or Pizza Hut, pizza in Naples is served either as rectangular slices or as a disc that's just large enough to cover a dinner plate.

Classic Neapolitan Pizza Margherita. Photo by Valerio Capello at English Wikipedia, CC BY-SA 3.0

We've already talked about the small, round version that is pizza Napoletana. Roman pizza is known for being long, rectangular, and may have a thinner, crispy crust. No one's going to feed you to the lions for making it in an electric oven, either. Plus, the rectangular shape means it's more easily cut to whatever size the customer desires.

Roman Pizza. Photo by Shoebill2, Public domain, via Wikimedia Commons

In Sicily, pizza is traditionally square and has thicker dough and more sauce and cheese than that of Naples. (a stretched-curd cow's or sheep's cheese), onions, breadcrumbs, and a touch of anchovies are what you'll find on Sicilian pizzas. As with other

Sicilian Sfincione Pizza. Photo by Rino Porrovecchio, CC BY-SA 2.0 via Wikimedia Commons

19

Totally Pizza

A pizza being made in Mozzaluna's wood-fired oven. Photo by johnmleclaire, via Wikimedia Commons

parts of Italy, pizza style is determined by whatever locally grown ingredients are available. The basic format may be similar all over a region like Sicily, but will often differ by city.

Ovens: Wood, Coal, or Gas? That is the Question

If you really want to do Naples-style pizza right, you need a wood-burning brick baking oven. That's how the old 16th century pizzaiolos did it, and that's how their descendants still bake pizza.

Genuine New York pizza? Now you're talking coal ovens. Oh, and if you're actually in New York, you'll need to buy a place that already has one, since the city outlawed new coal-burning overs years ago, and the only ones operating now were grandfathered in.

For restaurants, there are many options for baking pizza. Want to be a traditional? Try a coal- or wood-burning oven with stone bricks above the heat source. Need to get high volume out quickly for delivery? A conveyor belt oven is probably better for you. With deck ovens, you can slide the pizza directly onto the bricks with a pizza peel.

Homemade pizza chefs have a variety of options too. Any kitchen oven will cook frozen or take-and-bake pies just fine. If you're into scratch-built pizza, you can bake on a pizza stone to emulate the effect of baking on the stones in a brick oven. My personal favorite is grilling pizza on my barbecue grill out back.

Totally Pizza

Quiz

Question: Bakers often use a shovel-like peel to slide bread, pizza, and other baked goods into and out of their ovens. Which of the following is most likely the root derivative for the peel's name?

A. Portuguese: *pele*

B. English: peel

C. French: *pelle*

D. Greek: *pelio*

Correct Answer: C. French: *pelle*, which describes a shovel as well as a peel.

Pizza: Great Any Way You Slice It

We're all familiar with the stereotypical wheel pizza cutter—a simple device that does the job. Me, though, I'm more partial to the mezzaluna cutter. First, chicks dig the word "mezzaluna" a lot more than "pizza wheel." Which would you rather hear on a romantic night in of homemade artisan pizza, ladies? "I just love my pizza wheel." Or, "Would you like to see my mezzaluna? I only take it out on special occasions."

Even the translation sounds a little romantic. Mezzaluna is Italian for "half moon." That's exactly what a mezzaluna looks like, too. It's a large curved blade with handles on each end or across the spine that you roll back and forth across the pizza to cut it up. The double-bladed version is often used to mince herbs or chop vegetables, too.

Mezzalunas were first used in the 18th century. They were invented by Silvio Pacitti in 1706. Some types of mezzalunas (particularly the double-bladed type) are

Mezzaluna pizza cutter, Photo by CTHOE, CC BY-SA 3.0 via Wikimedia Commons

often used to mince herbs or chop vegetables. Tell your date that with the right words and lighting and she may be impressed by your knowledge of Italian culinary history. Say it wrong, though, and you're just some pizza-obsessed screwball with a big knife. It's all in the delivery.

Part II

American Pie

Pizza and Bongos was part of a series of international albums by Irving Fields. It naturally featured Italian music. Fields was a pianist and lounge artist who lived to be over a hundred. Courtesy of Internet Archive.org

 Once Upon a Time in America

Pizza isn't as fundamental to Italy as it is to America. Over there, it plays a second-ary role to pasta, risotto, and polenta. To be candid, I think they could do without it. Not us. Over here, it's one of the few foreign foods we've embraced wholeheartedly, made entirely our own. —Alan Richman, 'American Pie: The 25 Best Pizzas You'll Ever Eat', *GQ* (May, 2009)

Queen Margherita gave pizza her legendary blessing, Rome gave it a thin crunchy crust, but the American business machine gave it to the world, via mass production and some very creative takes on the food's simple for-mula. Old-country Neapolitans hated the idea of homogenous, white bread pizza produced in assembly-line fashion, like cars in a factory. You can understand their panties being in a twist on that point. However, they also frowned on anything else that wasn't considered to be pizza made in the Neapolitan tradition. The Chicago deep dish and Hawaiian pizzas that we know and love were the hated bastard chil-dren of the pizza family in their eyes.

Interestingly, pizza's early history here in the United States is more similar to its Italian origin story than the Neapolitans would like to admit. Much like in Italy, it was a regional food until after WW II. The region in this case, though, was wherever Nea-politan immigrants settled down—mostly the Northeastern United States, in places like New York and New Haven. I know what you're thinking, but no, Italians didn't choose New York because they really wanted to see *Les Mis* or *Phantom*. It just so happens that Europe is closer to Ellis Island than to San Francisco Bay. Seeing as how the last thing I want when I come off of a five-hour plane trip is a nice long walk, I can only imagine how little an immigrant wants to keep moving after spending weeks at sea.

There was a big immigrant push from Italy to the United States that started in the late 1800s. You know those poor, huddled masses you hear about when you tour the Statue of Liberty? Yep, that was these folks—about five billion of them. Many were looking to snag one of the factory jobs that arose in the American Northeast,

Totally Pizza

Italian immigrants on the way to Ellis Island, 1905. Photo by Lewis W. Hine, Public Domain image

while others were looking to work with relatives who were already here. Some of these newcomers were Neapolitans, who—of course—brought their cuisine with them. Much like in Naples, pizza was mostly a street food for the blue-collar crowd and the poor. This totally makes sense, since the poor were the ones moving here. Lady Liberty invited them, after all.

Lombardi's Pizzeria in Brooklyn. Public Domain image

No one can say for certain who made the first pizza stateside, but we do know who opened the first pizzeria with a business license. That would be Neapolitan immigrant Gennaro Lombardi in New York City, 1905. He came to America in 1897 and set up shop as a grocer and baker. Pizza was a side product of that business until it gained enough popularity to stand on its

26

own (more on Gennaro in the next chapter). Over the next three decades, *pizzaiolos* opened up shop along the northeast coast, several of whom received their training at Lombardi's pizzeria. Some scattered pizzerias sprang up as far away as San Francisco during this time, but for the most part, American pizza spent its early childhood in the East or in Chicago.

The Doughy Spoils of War

Following that little misunderstanding called World War II, pizza in America hit adolescence. Like an awkward teenage boy, it got bigger, and strange ingredients started showing up on it, like so much "hair in new places." This is when pizza's family tree started to really branch off.

American GI's loved pizza after trying it in Campania during the war, so they hunted it down upon their return to the United States. Those pizza lovers who couldn't find a pizzeria tried making it at home, with mixed results. As pizza picked up steam and spread like a culinary virus (albeit a benevolent one), businessmen saw the opportunity to turn America's desire for the darling of Naples into serious coin. They started offering it at street fairs, and pizza joints became more family-friendly as opposed to the pre-war pizzerias that were open late and also sold alcohol. Food writers promoted it as simple, fun food. Home chefs and pizzeria owners alike brought their creativity into redefining pizza according to their tastes, or—in the case of the business owners—what they thought would stand out in the market. Just as pizza evolved during its spread across Italy, the same phenomenon took place in the states. People experimented with pizza almost as soon as they tried it, making things like English muffin pizza. In America, tossing pineapple and ham into the mix was considered fun and innovative. In Naples, it was grounds for excommunication.

The first thing G.I. Joe did after winning WWII and changing into his civvie tweeds was head out for pizza with his girl. Public Domain image

Totally Pizza

As Europe was rebuilding itself, the US helped out via the Marshall Plan from 1948 to 1952. Since the US and Canada were the only two economic powers untouched by the war, they were able to export goods and services to the devastated countries where the war took place. That meant huge economic growth for the United States, which translated into a lot of available jobs. With both men and women going to work, people looked for faster, more convenient ways to feed their families. As it turns out, a big chunk of flatbread covered in meat and cheese did the job rather nicely. Pizza still fed the poor masses, but it fed the rising middle class as well.

American Pizza Grows Up Fast and Easy

The first wood-fired brick pizza oven on the West Coast went into business in 1935 when the Cantolupo family opened their little Italian restaurant on Kearny Street. The Cantolupos were immigrants from Naples who gave many San Franciscans their first taste of pizza during and after World War II. GI's and their families crowded into the restaurant, filling wooden booths where newspapers served as tablecloths. A small pizza cost .75¢ and Veal Scaloppini $1.50. In 1971 the family retired and gave the restaurant to their long-time chef, Tommy Chin, who had come on board in 1936. When Tommy Chin took over he decided to change the name to an Italianate version of his own name and Lupo's became Tommaso's. It's still in business today.

Ike Sewell started Pizzeria Uno in Chicago in 1943, offering a thick crust and a wider variety of toppings that were geared toward Midwestern tastes. His version was baked in a frying pan instead of on a flat baking tray or oven floor. Some consider this the birth of the deep-dish pizza. Not only did it draw droves of customers, but copycats too. Competitors opened deep-dish pizzerias all over the Illinois area. Compare the tomato pie and deep-dish to the Rennaissance-era *torta*.

By the 1950s, pizza was leaving America's Little Italy pizzerias and migrating to the mainstream. Frozen pizza, store-bought pizza kits, and pizza chains were all born in that decade. Unlike the handmade pizzas crafted in mom-and-pop pizzerias, these mass-produced pizzas lacked the feel of Old World craftsmanship (an incredible understatement). However, much like with a favorite hooker or a favorite beer, you always knew what to expect with standardized pizza. Though there were some health scares with frozen pizza early on, for the most part they were safe, cheap, convenient fast food. Dean Martin showed pizza some love as early as 1953 in his hit song *That's Amore*. While the song was meant to evoke the Old Country, the term "pizza pie" originated in the United States.

Pizza's popularity continued to grow. Busy Americans could get it frozen at the supermarket, buy it in kit form, or pick one up from a pizzeria on the way home after

Totally Pizza

work. Roman Pizza Mix was the first home pizza kit, launched in 1948 out of Worcester, Massachusetts. It was the brainchild of Frank Fiorillo. Come the 1960s, you could use a little device called a telephone* to order one and have it delivered to your house. Some credit Domino's founder Tom Monaghan with introducing America to that concept, but whoever the originator was, they probably regret not getting a patent on the idea. By 1970, pizza was the second most popular fast food in the United States. Only the cheeseburger had more fans.

American pizza went through an identity crisis in the 1980s with the rise of gourmet pizza. Think of it as the "I just experimented a little in college" phase. California chefs used the middle-class staple as a canvas for the culinary arts. Alice Waters fired up the oven at Chez Panisse Café, making organic pizzas with locally-grown ingredients. When Wolfgang Puck hired Ed LaDou as the pizza chef at his famous Los

Chef Boy-ar-dee ushered in the era of kit pizza. Vintage advertisement circa 1964

Totally Pizza

Angeles restaurant Spago in 1982, the new chef gave pizza the high-end treatment, using toppings like roast duck, truffles, smoked salmon, and goat cheese. This isn't to say the big pizza companies sat on their collective butts. In the mainstream, Domino's made a huge push across the United States, guaranteeing delivery in 30 minutes or less, or your pizza was free.

At this point, you could say American pizza was all grown up. It had gone out into the great big world, had some wild experiences, and now it just needed to come back home and apologize to mom and dad for its obnoxious teenage years. In a desire to return to pizza's culinary roots, people started looking into traditional pizzerias as an alternative to standardized fare and its crazy cousin, the gourmet pizza. As often happens with a trend, that which was old became new again. People made (and still make) pizza pilgrimages to places like Lombardi's. Others, like Chris Bianco, traveled all the way to Naples and became AVPN-certified *pizzaiolos* to bring that tradition back home to the States.

Now that pizza is positively mainstream, it has its very own trade show. Every March, you can go to the Pizza Expo in Las Vegas. Not only is it an industry show, you'll also find pizza games, contests, and seminars. And any self-respecting food product needs to have its own month. Somewhere, some genius in Congress came up with the greatest idea ever—designating October as National Pizza Month. Since beer and pizza is the world's happiest couple, celebrating pizza during Oktoberfest makes huge sense. And it's not a great leap to use bratwurst instead of Italian sausage on your pie.

*It's that thing with the cord and the round circle with holes that old people used to call each other with in the Dinosaur Age of the 1900s.

Holiday Shopping

Which of the following is *not* one of the five top days for pizza sales each year in the United States?
New Year's Eve
Super Bowl Sunday
Halloween
New Year's Day
The night before Thanksgiving
Valentine's Day
Answer: (F) Valentine's Day. Are you kidding? Give your woman a pizza for Valentine's Day and see what happens, Romeo. Or more to the point, *doesn't* happen.

Totally Pizza

American Pizza By the Numbers

1957: the year Celentano Brothers launched the first nationally-marketed brand of frozen pizza

93 percent: The number of Americans have eaten pizza in the last month. And we wonder why there's an obesity problem in this country.

46: The average number of slices consumed by each American, annually.

61,000: The number of pizzerias in the U.S.

5 billion: The number of pizzas sold around the world, three billion of them in the US. Suck on that, McDonald's.

36 percent: The number of Americans who consider pizza the perfect breakfast. The other 64% are wrong.

100: the number of acres that would be covered by the pizza Americans consume annually. As if pizza actually grows on a farm. Who comes up with this stuff?

350: The slices per second we Americans scarf every year (burp!).

62 percent: The number of Americans who prefer meat over veggies on their pizza.

55: Pizza boxes the average pizzeria uses in a day.

$4 Billion: The value of cheese used by the pizza industry annually.

Quiz
Which of the following was the first pizzeria to go into franchising?
Domino's
Pizza Hut
Pizza the Hutt
Shakey's
Chuck E. Cheese

Answer: (D) Shakey's, in 1954. Pizza Hut didn't open until 1958, Domino's wasn't started until 1960, Pizza the Hutt was a character in Space Balls, and Chuck E. Cheese wasn't inflicted on parents' wallets until 1977. Shakey's was named after co-owner Sherwood "Shakey" Johnson who'd suffered nerve damage stemming from a wonderful run in with malaria he experienced during World War II. It could have been worse, though. Just imagine if it was erectile dysfunction. No one wants to buy a pizza from "Softy's."

Totally Pizza

The Six Million Dollar Pan

You'd think the highest-grossing indie pizzeria in the country would be in New York or Chicago, but it isn't. It's in my hometown of Anchorage, Alaska. The Moose's Tooth Pub and Pizzeria has about $6 million in annual sales. The most expensive pizza I've eaten in the state, though, was during a fishing trip north to Nome. A large pizza there goes for $35. That's what happens when it costs a bundle to ship (or fly in) all of your ingredients. More on Moose's Tooth in chapter 14.

Not to be outdone by my fellow Alaskans, Award Winning Chef Renato Viola in Italy makes what has been dubbed "The World's Most Expensive Pizza." His Louis XIII pizza costs $12,000. Not only that, making it takes a tad longer than sticking it in a brick oven for six minutes. Like, 72 hours. Your twelve grand doesn't just get you a pizza; it gets you an entire experience (which it should). See, when you place your order, a pizza chef, sommelier, and exclusive limited-edition cutlery and plates arrive at your home in Italy to make the thing. That said, the crust is made 72 hours ahead of time. Each Louis XIII is topped with a red carpet event of ingredients. Three types of caviar, eight cheese varieties (including organic buffalo mozzarella), Australian pink salt from the Murray River, mantis shrimp, prawns from Cilento, and lobster adorn its doughy surface. Oh, and it's accompanied by Remy Martin Cognac Louis XIII and a bottle of vintage 1995 Krug Clos du Mesnil champagne. At that price, they all better be at daddy's place in under thirty minutes or Big Poppa's gonna cut somebody. You feel me?

The Louis XIII "Very Expensive Pizza" courtesy of renatoviola.com

 New York Pizza: The Passion of the Slice

"Here's the most significant difference between New York pizza and Neapolitan pizza: you eat it [Neapolitan pizza] with a knife and fork! You don't see people picking up the slice. Kooky, right? Everybody talks about crust, but at the end of the day I think, everybody's pizza box or plate ends up looking pretty similar...all of the sauce and cheese eaten out of the center. And who gets left alone, shivering with frustration? The crust. Like Jeremy Piven in a strip club."
— *Anthony Bourdain from his program* No Reservations

What separates New York style pizza from other American styles is its thin, hand-tossed crust made from high-gluten bread flour. New York pizza dough is soft, silky, and bakes into a thin, chewy pizza. It's topped with tomato sauce and mozzarella cheese. Traditionalists eat it folded. New York-style pizza is usually sold both by the slice and/or as whole pies, depending on how old-school the joint is. Slices are commonly made from an 18-inch pie and cut into eighths. There's also a square variant of the slice made with a thicker dough, called a Sicilian slice. Some places that offer both refer to the normal style as "Neapolitan" pizza. Neither one bears all that much similarity to its Old World cousin.

No one has done more for New York pizza, and perhaps American pizza, than Gennaro Lombardi, or as I like to think of him, Pizza Jesus. Think about it: both spread a cultural concept to the masses, both had disciples, both worked miracles with bread, and neither could have seen just how far future generations would take their work. I know that's blasphemous, but come on, do you really think Jesus envisioned the Popemobile?

I always knew I was a slacker as a teen, but I didn't know just how much of a sloth boy I was until I found out about Gennaro Lombardi. Not only did he immigrate to the United States to start a new life, he was age 14 at the time. He worked days in the grocery store beneath his apartment in return for room and board, while working nights as a baker in Brooklyn. He was seriously hardworking and energetic—and

33

Totally Pizza

apparently required zero sleep. Making money as a grocer was tough, so he supplemented his income by baking pizzas and extra bread at night at the bakery and selling it the next day at the grocery store. And I thought I had it rough cleaning up after the family dog.

Apparently, he sold a shitload of those pizzas, because at 17, he took over the grocery business from the previous owner and bought the building. Lombardi expanded the business by selling pizza *and* bread to Italian factory workers operating in the Soho area. A few years later, he abandoned the bakery side of the business for the much more lucrative pizza trade. He licensed the pizzeria in 1905. It was pretty basic—a coal-fired oven with some tables and chairs. The fare was basic too: you could get any ingredient you wanted on your pizza, so long as it was San Marzano tomatoes and/or mozzarella cheese. Gennaro wrapped them in paper that was tied shut with string. Pizza was sold by the piece, not the slice (meaning the pieces varied in size and shape, rather than the pies being uniformly cut). The type of customer dictated price; a piece ran between 1 to 5 cents, with a portion to match. According to legend, the seriously poor could sneak in to snatch the leftover crusts of others. Lombardi's dough was too delicate for tossing and had to be hand-stretched until it was very thin.

The tile front of the original coal-fired pizza oven from Lombardi's 1905 pizza joint is still in service today. By Joe Hall from Takoma Park, MD, USA via Wikimedia Commons

Totally Pizza

Eventually success came and brought with it his nickname: Don Gennaro. He was a caring guy who helped out in the community—sort of like Don Corleone, without the horse's head. A lot of young guys coming over from Naples stopped in at Lombardi's. Some stayed to work—they were given room and board upstairs and sponsorship in the United States in exchange. After a few years they'd go off on their own, opening their own pizzerias and spreading the Pizza Good Word in the process.

Working for Lombardi was no joke. The joint was open from 7 a.m. to 4 a.m. every day and the clientele ran the gamut from poor to wealthy. During the day, neighbors, kids, and housewives all stopped by for a cut, while the night crowd was similar to today's club crowd after hours. Some of the night owls were pretty famous, too. Gennaro Lombardi counted opera star Enrico Caruso among his regulars.

After WWII, people began to move out of the old neighborhood to the 'burbs. The Soho factories moved their businesses to New Jersey. Other ethnicities moved in. While pizza in general spread around the country, the demand for whole pies in parts of New York fell off.

That's how pizza-by-the-slice came to be. The fast-paced workforce demanded an equally expedient lunch, and pizza didn't meet that requirement the way burgers and sandwiches did. Someone got the idea to make a circular (as opposed to just rounded) pizza and sell it by the slice. Throw in a pizza chef working near the shop's window, and you have free advertising to boot. Today there are over 9,000 pizza joints in New York alone. You could say there was a pizza Renaissance.

In 1984, the original Lombardi's closed. However, New York's pizza public wouldn't stand for it. People missed Lombardi's, pressure mounted, and the place was reopened yet again in 1994. The current incarnation opened thanks to Gennaro's grandson Gerry Lombardi, wife Josephine, and John Brescio. The old coal-fired oven had collapsed in the interim, so they relocated down the road in an old bakery at 32 Spring Street. Like the original location, it had a coal-fired baker's oven. They even took the time to transplant the old tiles from the dead oven to the face of the new one. The new oven is a great fit; just like its predecessor, it heats up to 900 degrees F., holds about 7 pizzas, and cooks them in 3 1/2 minutes.

Back in the pollution-happy toddlerhood of the Industrial Revolution, coal was the way to go for anything requiring heat. "Just keep shoveling," factory foremen would say. "Never mind all of that coughing and the watery eyes, you pantywaist. It builds character." In the American northeast, bakers loved themselves some coal-fired ovens. That transferred over to pizza, of course, and became part of what gives vintage Big Apple pizza its distinct flavor. Coal ovens generate a pizza crust that tends to be a little charred and has a smoky flavor. It's very dry in the coal oven, making

Totally Pizza

for a light and crunchy crust. Gas ovens became more and more popular because they were easier and cheaper to operate. Over 50 years ago, the use of coal ovens was outlawed in New York City. Fortunately, old pizzerias and bakeries got grandfathered in. That's why you can still get the smoky goodness old school Big Apple pizza is known for.

"A magnificent conglomeration of black-and-white enameled bricks on the outside and terra-cotta bricks on the inside. Tons of heat-retaining sand lie below. It is about seven feet high and twelve feet across and twelve feet deep. It can hold fifteen pizzas at once."

—Herbert Mitgang, 'Pizza a la Mode', *New York Times* (12 February 1956), describing the pizza oven at Lombardi's

The Disciples

Unlike the biblical messiah, no one can say for certain just how many disciples Gennaro Lombardi had during his long career spreading the Gospel of Pizza. What *is* known are which of the famous Big Apple *pizzaiolos* got their start at Lombardi's back in the day, and when. The three apostles of pie founded the three most legendary pizzerias in New York after Lombardi's—John Sasso, Anthony Pero, and Patsy Lancieri.

Anthony Pero: In 1905, Anthony "Totonno" Pero started working at his old friend Gennaro Lombardi's pizzeria in New York. By 1924, he'd saved enough to branch out on his own. Pero opened his own pizzeria on Coney Island called Totonno's. It's not only known for its classic New York pie, but also for its long life and lines out the door. Pero struck out on his own

Would the real Patsy's Pizzeria please stand up? Patsy's Pizzeria in East Harlem, New York City. Photo by Paul Lowry from New York via Wikimedia Commons

shortly after the subway started running out to Coney Island, bringing opportunity with it. They've made their pizza the same way since 1924. Legend has it that Anthony could be ruthless with his customers. If the Totonno's owner got a pizza complaint from a customer, he confiscated the pie and told the offender to beat it. Not only that, he also only made a certain amount of dough each day, when it was gone, you were shit out of luck. You could say he was an early incarnation of the Soup Nazi from *Seinfeld*.

John Sasso: John's Pizzeria was founded in 1929 by John Sasso on Bleecker Street , and the restaurant is still in its original location. They serve coal-fired, brick oven pizza made to order, cooked in 850-degree ovens. Seating is in traditional, timeworn booths, surrounded by celebrity photos and New York memorabilia. When John Sasso left Lombardi's to open John's Pizzeria in Greenwich Village, he decorated the place with a sign that read simply, "No Slices," apparently to distinguish his joint from Patsy's Pizzeria.

Pasquale "Patsy" Lancieri: Following his alleged work at Lombardi's Lancieri founded Patsy's Pizzeria in East Harlem in 1933. Although its history gives the joint plenty of street cred, Patsy's biggest claim is as the origin of pizza by the slice.

Patsy Lancieri died in the 1970s and his widow sold the East Harlem pizzeria to longtime employees in 1991, much to the dismay of her nephew Patsy Grimaldi, who, well, felt like a patsy. He retaliated by opening a Patsy's in Brooklyn. The feuding deepened when Greek pizza man Nick Tsoulos and wife, Mirene, opened six Patsy's Pizzerias in Manhattan. Patsy Grimaldi changed the name of his pizzeria to Grimaldi's, which the *New York Times* said is the best and truest to the original.

In 2009 there was another legal battle between Patsy's Pizzeria and Patsy's Restaurant on West 56th Street, founded by Pasquale (Patsy) Scognamillo in 1944, which was a haven for Frank Sinatra and many celebrities. Will the real Patsy please stand up?

Somebody Just Took a Bite Out of Grandma

In 1965 Umberto Cortero started a pizzeria called Umberto's of New Hyde Park on Long Island. He later was joined by his brother, Carlo, and they'd make "grandma pizza" for themselves. Friends urged him to put it on the menu but he refused because he felt another pizza on the menu would slow them down during a rush.

What exactly is grandma pizza, you ask? Surely it's not the end result of somebody's nana accidentally falling into the pizza oven. According to journalist Erica Marcus, who first wrote about grandma pizza in 2003 for *Newsday*, "Variations abound, but the basic outlines are as follows: a thin layer of dough is stretched into

Totally Pizza

Grandma pizza looks about as comforting as a quilt, if it were made of melted cheese and pepperoni over dough.
Photo by Jeffrey Tastes via Wikimedia Commons

an oiled, square "Sicilian" pan, topped sparingly with shredded mozzarella, crushed uncooked canned tomatoes, chopped garlic and olive oil, and baked until the top bubbles and the bottom is crisp. [Michele] Scicolone [Manhattan resident, Italian food expert, and co-author of *Pizza: Any Way You Slice It*] observed that grandma pie sounded a lot like 'pizza alla casalinga' (housewife-style pizza), 'the kind of pizzas you'd get in Italy if you were invited to someone's home.'"

Come the 1980s, their satellite restaurant, King Umberto's was sold to two employees who hired Ciro Cesarano and Angelo Giangrande as their pizza makers. It was they who saw the potential in grandma pizza and put it on the menu. The pie got another boost in 1989, when Giangrande took it to a pizza-making contest in Long Island where it was such a hit, the stuff was consumed before the competition even started! Although it hasn't managed to catch on as much as other types of pizza, grandma pizza's popularity has seen steady growth since the early 1990s.

On the Waterfront

Ask a native New Yorker what makes Gotham pizza so great and most will tell you it's the tap water in the dough. They have a harder time agreeing on what makes that water so special. Some sources say it's the mineral content of the water, others the quality of the copper pipes that carry it. Unlike their twenty-first-century counterparts, nineteenth-century politicians showed vision when setting up New York's water system. Instead of using the same local water sources that doubled as body dumps for

Totally Pizza

the Mafia, officials ordered an elaborate system of reservoirs and aqueducts to collect and deliver water from pristine watershed areas upstate.

Not only does New York's water system bless the city's nine million people with one billion gallons of fresh, clean water delivered from large upstate reservoirs each day, that water's unique characteristics are fought over in court by restaurants out-of-state. Two such joints in Florida claimed to capture New York tap water's distinct flavor and pass it along to their customers in bagels and pizza.

In its 2010 lawsuit, the Original Brooklyn Water Bagel Company (OBWBC) claims it created a process that "Brooklynizes" local water, and that Mamma Mia's Trattoria & Brick Oven Pizzeria in Lake Worth FL stole that technology.

Here's where it gets a little sticky. The pizzeria bought its water system from a third company, the Famous New York Baking Water Corporation, which was started by former employees of OBWBC, including the owner's father-in-law. Now you can see where OBWBC might have a case. For added drama, the pizzeria countersued, charging that OBWBC was making false claims about holding a patent on the method in order to keep others from cashing in on local demand.

At any rate, the process supposedly morphs garden-variety hard water into the soft water that New Yorkers drink from their taps (and which goes into NYC pizza dough). Visitors at the bagel joint can check out the equipment used to flush the water through the fourteen-step process. According to the blog gothamist.com "...if they really want to show who's got the most 'authentic' Brooklyn style, they should just skip the lawsuits and cut straight to burning down each other's businesses."

The Pizza Principle

In the 1980s, New Yorker Eric M. Bram noticed a relationship between the price of a slice of pizza and the cost of a New York subway token: they matched, and had matched, since the 1960s. This little theory, or as it's known now, Pizza Connection, has held true all the way to the present day, despite the discontinuation of subway tokens in favor of the MetroCard. New Yorkers have used prices of one to predict price increases of the other for years. And they're both *round*. Coincidence? I think not.

I mean, it does make cents when you think about it...A New York City Subway Token. Photo by Jessamyn West - Public Domain image.

Totally Pizza

Giants Fans and Blue Pie

Calling New York sports fans enthusiastic is like calling a wolverine irritable. Just check out what the owners of Joe's Pizza in Long Island did for their beloved New York Giants. When the team made it to the Super Bowl in 2012, the pizzeria stepped up to the line to congratulate the team with an honorary blue pizza. The pizza was a traditional white pizza, with some blue food coloring mixed in. *Pizza bianca* generally has no sauce, just a covering of mozzarella cheese on top of some garlic, olive oil and herbs, with whatever other toppings are involved. The pie was ringed with pepperoni for the red in the Giants colors. They also offered a pizza shaped like a football.

Pizza was happy to give 110% and would like to thank Jesus for making its victory possible as a reigning food MVP. Each Super Bowl Sunday in the United States, delivery sales spike on game day more often than any other during the year. It's not uncommon for delivery drivers to collect tips as high as $20 an order. Domino's drivers alone drive over 4 million miles that day.

 # The Pizza Belt

"We had a jukebox, and they'd be dancing in the aisles. We didn't serve lunch because I'd be here till 3:30 am. Some places did breakfast and lunch. We did dinner and craziness." —Nick Azzaro, Joe Papa's grandson, co-owner of Papa's Tomato Pies

Unlike its Iron and Bible counterparts, the Pizza Belt is pretty tasty. Writer Ed Levine coined the term in his book *Pizza: A Slice of Heaven.* The belt runs from Philadelphia into New York and New Jersey, as well as New Haven and Boston. Here's a list of the historic notables that formed it circa back in the day:

1910: Joe's Tomato Pies, Trenton, NJ

1912: Papa's Tomato Pies, Trenton, NJ

1925: Pizzeria Napoletana, New Haven, CT

1926: Pizzeria Regina Boston, MA

1927: Marra's, Philadelphia, PA

1932: Paul's Apizza, New Haven, CT

1934: State Street Apizza, New Haven, CT

1938: Sally's, New Haven, CT

If you ever decide you'd like to be drawn and quartered in Connecticut, just talk smack about Frank Pepe in New Haven. The man was a pizza legend, whose white apizza (pronounced "ah-beets" in the Neapolitan dialect) stands out in stark contrast to a classic New York pie (like the ones you'd find at Lombardi's or Patsy's). You can't talk about pizza history in the northeast without going into detail about Frank Pepe. It's not right, and might be illegal in Connecticut. After Lombardi and his ilk, Pepe was the most famous old-school *pizzaiolo* in the region.

Four years after Gennaro Lombardi got his business license and secured his place in pizza history, the seventeen-year-old Pepe migrated from Maiori in southern Italy

Totally Pizza

to New Haven, Connecticut to work in a factory. He learned a lot there...primarily, that he hated working in a factory. The Wooster Square area of New Haven where he lived wasn't the quaint historic community that it is now. Back then it was more of a—what's the term—shithole. Italians moved there because no one else wanted the place. No one deliberately surrounds themselves with tenements and factories unless they either own them or work there. That was the situation in Wooster Square in 1870 and into the early 20th century. This also tells you just how desperate people were to leave Italy. By some records, New Haven's Italian population numbered a whopping ten people in 1870. By 1910, it was 13,000. As more Italians moved in, Wooster Square got nicknamed "Little Naples." If you Google it, don't misspell it like I did. "Little Nipples" leads to something entirely different.

That's what awaited Pepe when he landed in New Haven. He was an uneducated, enthusiastic, hard-working immigrant like a lot of his fellow Italians. Once he'd had enough of the luxurious working conditions one encounters in a turn-of-the-century, soot-belching factory, he took a break to return home and fight for his country in a little spat called World War I. He learned another lesson during this time—that war is about as much fun as working in a soot-belching, turn-of-the-century factory.

After the war, he returned to New Haven—only this time, Frank got a much happier gig at a bakery on Wooster Street. He also started walking the Wooster Square market, selling tomato pies from a specially built rack he wore on his head. Frank made good money doing that, but unlike me in my youth, he didn't blow it all on strippers in Las Vegas. Pepe squirreled it away until he eventually bought out the bakery and turned it into the very first Frank Pepe Pizzeria Napoletana on June 16, 1925. It was the birth of a pizzeria dynasty. According to some accounts, Frank had a habit of smacking bad customers with his long wooden pizza peel. He probably didn't enjoy it as much as that creepy frat guy who spanked Kevin Bacon in *Animal House*, though.

Frank Pepe gave the world the white pizza that sets New

The exterior of Frank Pepe Pizzeria in New Haven, CT. Photo by Krista, CC BY 2.0, via Wikimedia Commons

Totally Pizza

Haven apart from pies in the rest of America. When he first started out, Pepe only made two varieties of pizza. As it turned out, he was allergic to both. One had oregano, chopped garlic, tomato sauce, and grated pecorino romano cheese, while the marinara version sported tomato sauce, grated cheese, and anchovies. You won't find tomatoes or mozzarella on a white pizza. The toppings you *will* get are grated cheese, chopped garlic, oregano, olive oil, and littleneck clams.

White Clam Pizza in New Haven, Connecticut . Photo by ZhengZhou, CC BY-SA 4.0, via Wikimedia Commons

Although the business was Frank's, the land belonged to the Boccamiello family, who kicked him out to start their own pizzeria on that spot called—ironically—The Spot. Pepe re-opened his place right next door in 1936. That's where the clams come in. There was an alley between the two pizzerias. Bear Boccamiello used that space to shuck and sell clams on the half shell. That led to Pepe's restaurant serving littleneck clams on the half shell at the bar. Eventually, Frank decided to put the clams on the pizza, and white apizza was born. It takes three Pepe's employees to give a shuck. At least, that's how many it takes to shuck the clams onsite.

Rival pizzerias continued to spring up. Modern Apizza opened its doors in 1934. In 1938, Frank's nephews Sal and Tony Consiglio left their uncle's employ to strike out on their own just down Wooster Street with Sally's Apizza. Pepe's and Sally's have a friendly competition that continues to this day.

Modern Art

Not all of New Haven's historic pizzerias are on Wooster Street. Modern Apizza, the third leg of New Haven's triad of famous pizzerias, opened up 75 years ago as State Street Apizza on—surprise, surprise, State Street. It's been in the same East Rock neighborhood ever since. In 2011, Adam Richman dropped by during the first episode of Man v. Food Nation.

Like the Wooster Street pizzerias, Modern serves New Haven-style thin-crust apizza. The biggest difference is the oven. Pepe's and Sally's use coal-burning brick ovens, but Modern heats their pies in an oil-fueled brick oven. Just like their rivals, the restaurant sells Foxon Park soft drinks, made locally in East Haven, Connecticut. Although Clams Casino may sound like the name of a gambling den from Spongebob Squarepants, it's actually a Modern Apizza specialty pizza topped with bacon, clams, and peppers. They also make a white tuna pie. Modern Apizza uses fresh littleneck clams for their white clam pies. The only difference between Modern and Pepe's is that Modern uses pre-shucked clams. In 2010 Modern Apizza earned a spot on playboy.com's Best Pizza in America top ten list.

Jersey Tomato Pie, Tacconelli's, and Rhode Island Strip Joints

The signature move in Jersey is tomato pie, especially in Trenton. Unlike New York pizza, which has an obvious Neapolitan influence, Trenton tomato pie takes its styling cues from Sicilian pizza. Unlike other versions of pizza around the country, tomatoes don't take a back seat to other toppings. In fact, a properly made tomato pie first has cheese sprinkled over a thick, focaccia-like crust, then the whole shebang is crowned with crushed, seasoned plum tomatoes. Like Sicilian pizza, tomato pie is baked in a large aluminum pan and served in square slices.

Depending on what person you ask, Trenton is home to either the oldest or the second oldest pizzeria in the United States. Some people (probably the ones from Jersey) say that Papa's Tomato Pies, which opened in 1912, is the oldest pizzeria in the country because unlike Lombardi's, it never closed down. Yes, anal-retentive New Jersey pizza zealots, Papa's is the oldest *continually operated* pizza joint in the United States. But Gennaro Lombardi still beat NJ's Joe's Tomato Pies, the second old-

est pizzeria in the country, to the punch by five years. Deal with it. Joe's opened in 1910. Food writer Ed Levine, in his book, *Pizza: A Slice of Heaven*, called Trenton "one of the oldest notches on the Pizza Belt."

Two years later, Papa's Tomato Pies opened up on South Clinton Avenue. Like Lombardi and Pepe, Joe Papa was 17 years old when he started his own

Papa's Tomato Pies, the oldest continually-operated pizza joint in the United States, opened in 1912.
Photo courtesy of Pizzahalloffame.com

Totally Pizza

business. He came over from Naples several years before, moved to Chambersburg (Trenton's Little Italy), and eventually found himself working at Joe's Tomato Pies. Much like in other parts of the northeast, Papa's kept long hours, staying open until 3 AM to catch hungry factory workers getting off work and equally famished bar goers in need of a bite after hours.

Giovanni Tacconelli moved to Philadelphia from Italy in 1918, where he first worked as a laborer before returning to his native craft: baking. With the help of a few friends he built a 20x20-inch brick oven, surrounded it with dedication, and raised his family to work the business. That is, until World War II. With his sons drafted into the military, Tacconelli stopped baking bread. In 1946, he turned to creating tomato pies. The original Tacconelli's is still open in Philly, and the family has added a second location in Maple Shade, New Jersey. It's run by one of Giovanni's descendents, Vince Tacconelli, Jr.

Food writer Alan Richman wrote this about Tacconelli's pizza in his 2009 article for GQ entitled *American Pie: The 25 Best Pizzas You'll Ever Eat.* "Sometimes there is no explanation for great pizza. Sometimes there are no great ingredients in great pizza, no specially sourced mozzarella, no hand-harvested garlic. I come from Philadelphia, and I had never heard of Tacconelli's until recently, even though it was in business when I was growing up, going to school, and working there. What a wasted life."

Here's a little slice that a lot of the other pizza books miss: pizza strips. The bakery formerly known as Monda's in Providence, Rhode Island opened its brick ovens in 1918. By now you might begin to think pizza and baking may have some things in common. And you'd be right, Gump. The Monda family owned the bakery until brothers Arnold and Frank Buono bought it in 1989 with some help from their father-in-law,

Dan Amadio. I'm not saying pizza strips were invented here, but the place makes them. Hell, I'm not even saying pizza strips are real pizza. Pizza strips are basically strips of thick crust topped with tomato sauce and oregano. No cheese, no toppings. It figures that the smallest state in the Union would also have a pizza offshoot to match. They're a local product made by small bakeries. Some even make a white version.

Pizza strips are exactly what you think they are. Photo by David Iannotti, CC BY-SA 3.0, via Wikimedia Commons

Totally Pizza

Baking Soda

If you want the full New Haven pizza experience, you have to wash it down with Foxon Park bottled soda. When Frank Pepe opened up shop, Foxon Park was served side-by-side with his pies. The East Haven, Connecticut company started in 1922. Foxon Park was around when New Haven pizza was born, and has been ever since. Among the soda's more unique flavors are white birch, *gassosa* (an Italian lemon drink), and Iron Brew, which is big in Ireland. If you want to wimp out and be normal, Foxon Park also makes its own versions of sodas commonly found in the supermarket, albeit with cane sugar instead of high fructose corn syrup.

High Profile Pizza Lovers Quiz

Frank Sinatra and Ronald Reagan preferred which of the following New Haven pizzerias:

A. Frank Sinatra preferred Sally's
B. Reagan loved himself some Sally's
C. Sinatra was a Pepe's man
D. Reagan's choice was Pepe's
E. Neither man ever actually went to Connecticut

Answer: A. and D. Allegedly, Sinatra even went so far as to have Sally's pizzas picked up and delivered to him. Reagan's not the only president who was a Pepephile. The restaurant's website has several photos of Bill Clinton happily chowing down.

Famous Pizzafaces of New Haven

Which of the following celebrities has *not* visited the New Haven location of Frank Pepe Pizzeria Napoletana?

A. Robert DeNiro
B. Henry Winkler
C. Kelly Clarkson
D. Bill Murray
E. None of the Above

Answer: E. None of the Above. Not only have they all stopped by, so have John Turturro and Vince Vaughn, among others.

Uno, Due, Tre: Chicago's Deep-Dish Creators

"New Yorkers prove Chicago makes the better pizza every day. What's the first thing a New Yorker does when he gets a slice of pizza? He folds it to make it thicker. Like a deep-dish Chicago slice." —Attorney James Lockard, my good friend, a great gamer, and a fellow pizza enthusiast

Chicago and the Midwest are the missing links between New York's Old World pizza and what we know as "franchise" pizza. This is where Little Italy joined forces with Middle America to launch institutions like Pizza Hut, Domino's, Godfathers, Little Caesar's, and more.

If Gennaro Lombardi is the Jesus of American pizza, Ike Sewell and Ric Riccardo are its Romulus and Remus, only without the feel-good story elements of sucking a wolf's teat or fratricide. Like the fictional founders of Rome, they built an institution that spread widely and is alive to this day. They simply accomplished it with buttery dough and baking dishes instead of roads and legions. And—as far as I know—they never fed anyone to lions in an arena.

While Gennaro Lombardi was busy licensing his pizzeria, Ike Sewell spent his days learning to walk and not crap his pants, just like the rest of us do when we're toddlers. Sewell was born in 1903, 50 miles east of Dallas in the small town of Willis Point, Texas. That's right—he wasn't an Italian immigrant. You probably already figured that out, though. "Sewell" doesn't exactly scream Italian ancestry. He worked for American Airlines after college but moved to Chicago following the repeal of Prohibition, where he became a regional vice president of Fleischmann's Distilling Corporation.

Thank Goodness for Bad Mexican

In 1943, Ike and his business partner, Ric Riccardo* (born Richard Novaretti), opened Pizzeria Uno, giving the world Chicago deep-dish pizza in the process. And it all started with some really bad Mexican food.

47

Totally Pizza

Chicago already had pizza in its own Little Italy. What it lacked was good Mexican cuisine—like what you'd find in Sewell's home state of Texas. Correcting that travesty was Sewell's and Riccardo's intention going in. They leased the basement in an old mansion on Ohio and Wabash in Chicago's Near North side. A few bullfighting murals on the walls, and they were good to go.

Or so they thought. Dammit Jim, Sewell was a distillery executive, not a chef. And while Riccardo was already a restaurateur, he had absolutely no experience whatsoever with Mexican food. Lucky for us, neither did the Mexican bartender Sewell employed to cook a sample meal for them. The guy claimed he'd learned a thing or two growing up around his mother's kitchen. He may have, but none of it had anything to do with making good Mexican cuisine. In fact, Riccardo was given a violent case of food poisoning. Talk about blowing an interview.

Riccardo went back to the Old Country in the following months. His reasons for leaving vary, depending on the source (fighting in World War II, visiting his sick mother). According to Ike, Ric simply packed up and left the country with all of his cash. Following his return, however, he hit Ike with the idea of turning the basement space into a pizzeria. Sewell didn't exactly embrace the idea like a loving parent. While Ike didn't gain a nice case of Montezuma's Revenge from the thin-crusted Nea-

Pizzeria Uno, Chicago IL. Photo by Leandro Neumann Ciuffo, CC BY 2.0, via Wikimedia Commons

Totally Pizza

politan pie Riccardo made for him, pizza was nothing new in Chicago—and the pie wasn't filling enough for the big Texan. Popular legend has it that the two of them went into the kitchen to make something bigger, more "meat-and-potatoes" if you will, than a stock pizza. They (and/or their employees, depending on who you want to believe) came up with a buttery, thick crust loaded with an even thicker layer of cheese and other toppings. Their new invention practically required a fork and knife to get through it. Chicago deep-dish pie is usually 2-3 inches thick with a buttery, corn meal-dusted crust. The cheese sits under the toppings and the tomatoes.

That was how Pizzeria Uno and its legendary deep-dish, topping-heavy take on pizza came to be—according to the legend, anyway. Ike Sewell was certainly the Romulus of this story, but if that's the case, Ric Riccardo would be Remus, right? The Roman version of this story has Romulus whacking his brother after Rome is founded. Sewell certainly didn't knife his business partner. However, Riccardo did pass away in 1954, one year before Uno's sister joint, Pizzeria Due, opened its doors. That left Sewell as the sole front man for the business. In the years that followed, Ric's role in this slice of pizza history diminished as Ike took center stage.

The bottom line is this: Ike Sewell wasn't a pizza maker. He was a pizza *marketer*. In fact, he was so good at fronting pies that his name is the first that pizza buffs think of when it comes to Chicago-style deep-dish fare. In fact, his salesmanship may be what saved deep-dish pies from obscurity. Rome wasn't built in a day, and neither was Pizzeria Uno. Unlike Lombardi's or Pepe's, Uno didn't have a fan base in place when it opened as a pizzeria. What's more, it wasn't in Little Italy. People in Chicago didn't know what to make of the place. The few non-Italians who knew about pizza were put off by Uno's bizarre take on the dish, and Chicago's Italians were skeptical as well. No one beat down the doors on opening day...in fact, Pizzeria Uno almost went out of business.

Ike Sewell's marketing acumen carried Uno across this rough patch. He was personable, friendly, hard working, and took every opportunity he could to get people into the restaurant to try his deep-dished offering. Sewell even went so far as to give away free slices at the bar. That's when Chicago fell in love with it and eventually adopted deep-dish pizza into the city's identity. In 1955, Sewell opened a sequel pizzeria, Pizzeria Due, one block north of the original location.

*No relation to Lucy, Little Ricky, Fred, or Ethel.

Chicago Deep-Dish Goes Viral

Like Lombardi's and Pepe's, Uno was the mother ship that bred similar pizzerias via former employees opening their own versions of the original. Alice Mae Redmond

Totally Pizza

defected first. She was Uno's pizza chef and created a "secret dough conditioner" that went with her when she left. The soft-spoken Redmond teamed up with two cabbies named Sam Levine and Fred Bartoli as well as their buddy, George Loverde. Her partners wanted to open a deep-dish pie place but they were pizza virgins when it came to setting up operations. They had no idea what to do, but her guiding hand helped them out. She even brought in her sister, Ruth. The two women created the secret recipe for a deep-dish pizza that was the flagship pie for Gino's East, which opened in 1966 at 160 East Superior Street, just east of Michigan Avenue.

The next big exodus took place five years later. Rudy Malnati and his son Lou ran the day-to-day operations at Uno for years. It's even been put forth that Rudy was the guy who actually invented the deep-dish pizza for Sewell and Riccardo. Rudy, whose real first name was Adolfo, was Pizzeria Uno's bartender and Sewell's unofficial third partner in the business. His English was questionable but his loyalty to Ike wasn't. Neither was Lou's. They were the heart and soul of Uno for years.

That all changed when Lou, an ex-marine, pinned Ike down about that "unofficial partner" status with the pizzeria—not in the usual sense that one is pinned down by a United States Marine, however. All of Lou's suppressing fire was verbal. Nothing had been written down on paper, so Lou wanted to officially buy that part of the business he believed he and Rudy owned. Ike refused, and Lou struck out on his own. The two allegedly never spoke again.

Lou Malnati's Pizzeria first saw action on March 17, 1971. Chicago greeted it with a nice, long line down the street in Lincolnwood. Lou himself died from cancer seven years later but his sons Marc and Rick run the operation to this day. Not only did Malnati's make a great deep-dish pizza, it also introduced Chicago to something new—the pizzeria sports bar. On that first day back in 1971, customers found themselves surrounded by walls decked out in local sports paraphernalia like team jerseys. In 2004, Lou Malnati's grossed $3.5 million in FedEx-ed pizza sales alone. They must be doing something right.

All three pizzerias have branched into franchising since those days. No longer content with Pizzeria Uno and Due, Ike Sewell bred four clones in Massachusetts. He franchised the concept to the Uno Restaurant Holdings Corporation in 1979. Over the next ten years, the chain expanded like a real pizza-lover's waistline. One place where you won't find a lot of Pizzeria Uno's is, ironically, Chicago. The Windy City only has four of them—including Due and the original Uno in River North.

With more than 150 Uno Chicago Grill (as they're called now) locations in 24 states and assorted foreign countries, the chain is far and away the biggest of the Chicago triumvirate. Lou Malnati's ranks second, with more than 30 branches in the

Totally Pizza

Chicago area. Gino's East may only have 12 pizzerias, but the company sprinkled its restaurants around Illinois and into Wisconsin.

Pizza Hybrids: Stuffed, Pan, or Crunchy

Big shocker—Chicago also brought us stuffed pizza. In the mid-1970s Nancy's Pizza and Giordano's Pizzeria played around with deep-dish pizza. Nancy's founder Rocco Palese started it by basing the pie on his mom's *scarciedda* recipe. That's an Italian Easter tradition in the town of Potenza, Italy. Joseph and Efren Boglio worked for Nancy's as pizza chefs. When they left to open Giordano's, they took the concept with them. The dish gained popularity thanks to *Chicago* Magazine articles featuring Nancy's Pizza and Giordano's.

Stuffed pizza is the monster truck version of deep-dish. It's often deeper than a normal deep-dish and the toppings are much denser. Hey, it wasn't named "stuffed" because you buy it at the taxidermist.

Somewhere in Chicago, a deep-dish pizza and some focaccia went out, got drunk, hooked up, and produced a mutant hybrid. We're not sure if they called each other the next day or not, but what is known is that "pan" pizza has a thicker crust than normal deep-dish, with the toppings going on over the sauce instead of under it, much like with a normal thinner crust pie.

Stuffed pizza (family issues not shown). Photo by caribb, CC BY 2.0, via Wikimedia Commons

Unlike a New York thin-crust pizza, the Chicago version is thin and crisp enough to crunch when you bite it. It's also cut into squares or rectangles, aka "party cut" or "tavern cut." Aurelios is a chain that specializes in this kind of pizza.

Car Parts, Blind Pigs, and Detroit Pizza

Between the car industry, Motown Records, and the high crime rate, Detroit's history overshadows one of its other great contributions to American culture—Detroit-style pizza. It's a square-shaped affair featuring a deep-dish crust topped with pepperoni,

Totally Pizza

heaped with mozzarella, maybe more toppings, and then drizzled with tomato sauce. The shape is practical rather than aesthetic. In keeping with true Motor City style, the stuff is baked in auto parts assembly-line pans. The pans are square steel, and deeper than a typical deep-dish pizza pan. You can trace it back to Gus Guerra in 1946. By that time, he'd turned Buddy's Rendezvous, a Prohibition speakeasy (aka "blind pig" in the local lingo) into a legit operation. We all know American vets discovered European culture overseas and craved it when they got back home. Gus saw a chance to make his mark through pizza. He enlisted his wife, Anna, to prepare a special pizza dough borrowed from the recipes of her mother's Sicilian homeland. We're not sure where he got the idea for using a car parts container but you have to admit, the touch is definitely Detroit. These days, dozens of Motor City pizzerias make it, and it's even spread across the country to places like Austin and Colorado.

St. Louis Pizza: In A World of Its Own
Traditional St. Louis-style pizza is just about as far removed from the classic Neapolitan version as you can get. First off, it's founded on extremely thin, yeastless dough.

a freshly baked Imo's pizza at the Hampton and Oakland location. half Deluxe, half olive and canadian bacon. Public Domain image via Wikimedia Commons

Totally Pizza

When it's baked, the dough hardens into a texture that's closer to a giant cracker than what most people think of as normal pizza crust. Then there's the cheese—not only is it *not* mozzarella, it's a processed local blend called Provel.

Swiss, cheddar, and provolone comprise Provel cheese. Two competing entities take credit for its creation—the Sigillito family and Costa Grocery. Regardless, the name Provel is trademarked and dates back to the first half of the 20th century. The J.S. Hoffman Cheese Company of Wisconsin originally mass-produced it for the St. Louis market. Now, Kraft Foods owns it as a subsidiary, the Churny Company.

The more widely-accepted origin story holds that Tony Costa developed Provel in cahoots with the Hoffman Company during the early 1960s, and that the cheese was created specifically for St Louis pizza tastes. According to the Sigillito family, John Sigillito sold Provel at his downtown grocery store 20 years before Costa and the J.S. Hoffman Cheese Company began making it.

Regardless of who actually invented the stuff, Ed Imo gets the credit for Provel's successful career as a pizza topping. In 1964, Imo and his wife Marge started Imo's Pizza at Thurman and Shaw Avenues in St. Louis. The pizzeria was only open at night, offering pick-up and delivery. By day, Ed worked at his secret identity as a mild-mannered tile setter. Come the night, though, he donned an apron and turned into a pizza man. Their first kitchen wasn't exactly pimp—it consisted of a used oven, two refrigerators and a stove purchased for the princely sum of $75. Since opening day, Imo's has gone from a single store to more than 100 franchises. Each location uses 25,000 pounds of Provel a year.

Part III

Franchise Pizza

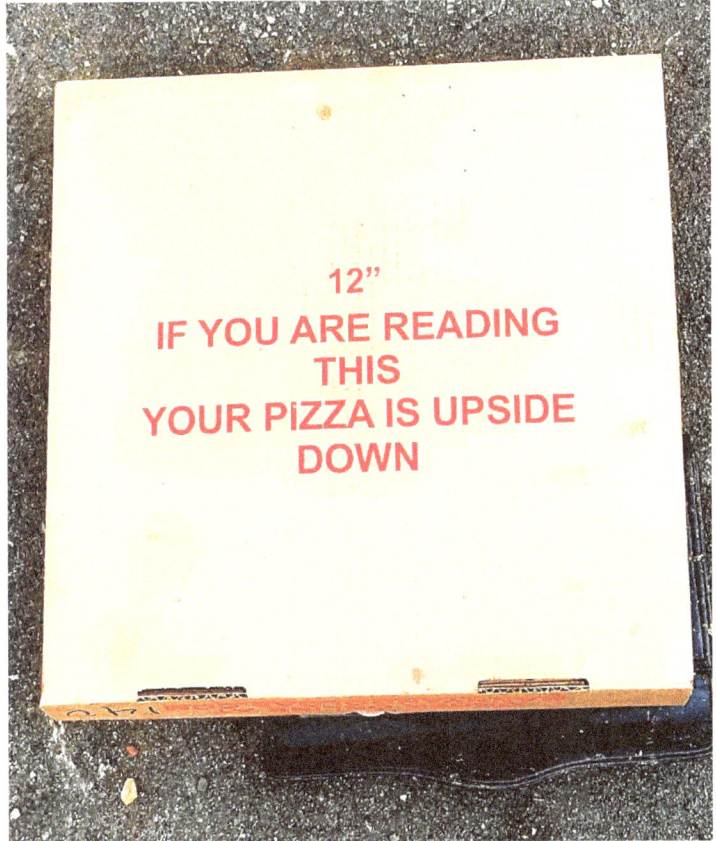

12"
IF YOU ARE READING
THIS
YOUR PIZZA IS UPSIDE
DOWN

Upside down pizza box. Photo by Mike Licht from Washington, DC, USA, CC BY 2.0, via Wikimedia Commons

Sex, Drugs, and the Rise of Corporate Pizza

"You can feed your face at any old place, but you can warm your heart at Shakey's."
—One of Shakey's old company slogans

Y ou want to know what really brought pizza into the mainstream? Sex. Popular theory holds that American GI's coming back after World War II launched the Italian food-of-the-gods out of Little Italy and onto Main Street. That's absolutely true. They didn't do it so much because of their taste buds as due to a part of the anatomy considerably lower down on the human body.

To hear many sources tell it, our vets magically discovered pizza in Italy like so many reverse Columbuses and sought it out when they got back Stateside. I'm certain some of them did, but were there really enough service personnel returning from Italy to explain pizza's huge explosion into the American consciousness in the 1950s and 1960s? Food writers argue whether or not that's the case. No one, however, disputes that soldiers returning from a war want to get laid, whether they're looking for life affirmation after facing so much death, or are just plain horny. World War II's wake saw the largest baby boom in the history of Western Civilization, especially in the United States.

During pizza's two-decade skyrocket to fame, all of those bundles of joy grew

Most folks who give a crap about such things think GI's created the demand for pizza. I'm not so sure. Public Domain photo

The spice, tang and sizzle of pepperoni pizza,

now in a mix.

Chef Boy-Ar-Dee

Chef Boy-Ar-Dee's pizza kits: the original take-and-bake.
Vintage magazine ad

into bratty toddlers, awkward tweens, and zitty teenagers, all of whom had to be fed if mommy and daddy wanted them to shut their whiny little pie holes. Their acne even gave rise to the colorful term, "pizza face." This population explosion started in the 1940s and continued into the 1960s, coinciding perfectly with the rise of franchise pizza (and other fast foods) across the U. S. and eventually the rest of the world.

Other sources tell us that mass production technology was really responsible for pizza's expansion in the 1950s and 1960s instead of the GI's. I don't see how that's possible, since factories *make* consumer products, they don't actually *use* them. Demand for convenient, tasty grub came first. Technology just rose to meet the need, just like it usually does. New innovations like the gas-heated conveyor oven and frozen food technology allowed corporate pizza to meet demand. While the Greatest Generation made franchise pizza, the Baby Boomers were the ones eating it.

Frozen pizza and home pizza kits like Chef Boyardee's were the gateway drugs that got the young Boomers hooked on pizza in the 1950s. Sometimes Mom and/or Dad also picked the stuff up from pizzerias on the way home to feed everyone after a long day. Later, Little Johnny and his pals ate the stuff while listening to that infernal rock n' roll racket.

And then the 1960s showed up...

...bringing pizza delivery with it. A lot of those kids went to college, some of whom experimented with recreational drugs that caused the munchies, Domino's targeted university campuses with pizza delivery, and you can figure out the rest, Sherlock.

Totally Pizza

All (most) kidding aside, home delivery revolutionized the pizza industry by offering fast food without the need to go and get it, let alone cook it. American life was faster than ever before and having food brought to your home, work, or dorm let you keep pace, whether you were studying hard, watching sports on TV with the guys, or just felt too tired to make dinner. Owning a car had grown so commonplace that pizza joints could hire drivers without having to buy a company car, making it a profitable business model, too.

By 1980 pizza franchises had gone international, bringing American-style pizza overseas. Domino's and Pizza Hut hit another growth spurt and grew even larger. The former through its "30 Minutes or Less or it's Free" delivery campaign and the latter because Pizza Hut shifted focus away from its sit-down model to the fast food and delivery-based business model we all know now. I can see why they did that, but I really miss the old pizzeria-esque Pizza Huts of my youth.

The `80s saw gourmet pizza get off the ground in California, and it spread out from there. Corporate pizza wasn't immune, either. While they don't carry organic barbecue goat cheese caviar pies, franchises have expanded their menus over the years to give consumers a greater variety from which to choose. What's more, the big pizza companies really go crazy with some of their offerings overseas. It's sort of like an executive with a bizarre fetish going to Thailand, only creative instead of creepy. Contrary to what a lot of Americans believe, the world doesn't revolve around our taste in food. Food corporations, with their legions of marketing folk, know that—and go to great lengths to figure out what other cultures want in products like pizza and then offer it to them.

The big downside to franchise pizza is that in some places it's done to indie pizzerias what Starbucks has done to small coffee houses—driven them out of business. In the short term, it stifled creativity and overshadowed the mom-and-pop feel created by the operations found in America's Little Italies by creating a standard pizza that's the same no matter where you get it. What most of the franchise companies share is a disconnection to pizza's cultural roots. It's a double-edged sword that freed them up to redefine pizza according to customer tastes, but by doing so they denied those same customers the experience of true Italian pizza as Naples intended; there's no cultural pride with corporate pizza. Any sane business owner does what they can to minimize costs; corporations just tend to be more extreme about it. In the case of pizza that means using wholesale ingredients instead of fresh or imported ones, with flavors to match. Generic in, generic out.

The rise of gourmet pizza led consumers to question what really defined pizza, and later on, to look for its roots again. The 1990s brought "artisan" pizza back into

Totally Pizza

the limelight,and while companies like Pizza Hut and Domino's didn't fall all over themselves designing a mass-produced New York-style pie for mass consumption, franchise companies have expanded into hot wings, pastas, dessert pizza, and offering a wider variety of pie. Vintage pizza's return to the spotlight caused some of pizza's old guard to open sequels or become small franchises themselves to meet the demand for classic, pre-WW II pizza.

The Music Man: Sherwood "Shakey" Johnson

I wasn't really shocked to find out that the same state that gave us Disneyland hosted the first pizzeria to turn franchise, Shakey's Pizza. In a way, Sherwood "Shakey" Johnson was Walt on a smaller scale. Both were creative guys who mixed music into their work. Johnson just preferred working with pizza instead of talking mice, angry ducks, and animators. Both, however, capitalized on the financial opportunities created by America's explosion of middle class families in the decades following World War II.

Shakey's had its opening day in Sacramento on April 30, 1954—a little over a year before ol' Uncle Walt launched Disneyland further south in Anaheim. Neither operation had a smooth opening day, either. When Disneyland had its first grand opening on July 17, 1955, it was as if Mickey had invaded the Bay of Pigs. Women's high heels sank in the still-tacky asphalt, none of the water fountains worked, and

Born a grocery store in its previous life, the first Shakey's stayed in business until the mid 1990s. Much like hair metal rock. Photo courtesy Shakey's Pizza USA, Inc.

Totally Pizza

ABC's live TV coverage was practically a blooper reel unto itself. Shakey Johnson only faced one big dilemma on opening day, though.

The pizza ovens didn't work.

You can see where that might be a slight problem for a pizza par-

Shakey Johnson teaching some poor schmuck in a bowler hat how to arrange pepperoni. Photo courtesy Shakey's Pizza USA, Inc.

lor. Unlike Disneyland, however, Shakey's did have working taps on opening day. The ovens hadn't been completed but the beer taps certainly were. It was the only thing served that weekend.

The following Monday saw Shakey Johnson and his business partner Big Ed Plummer turning the beer profits into pizza ingredients and Ye Public House for Pizza and Beer (as it was called) lived up to its full name. Johnson also used his restaurant as a chance to indulge his love of Dixieland jazz and ragtime music. Not just by forcing his employees to wear period uniforms guaranteeing no one would ever sleep with them, but by playing live music featuring player pianos and banjos. Customer sing-alongs and screenings of classic black-and-white comedy films were also part of the draw. Shakey even played some of that jazz piano himself to entertain diners.

By 1956, the idea had caught on enough for Shakey Johnson to make a sequel in Portland, Oregon. His third followed in 1959 in Albany, Oregon. Not only was it the first of the three pizza parlors where he actually bought the building, it was the first to feature the distinct architecture that defined the Shakey's building design (it now lives a quiet life as a used book store).

You'd think that the first pizza chain in America would also fall all over itself doing marketing research when it came to choosing new locations. Not so much. Johnson's company had a much simpler way of picking new locales—follow the shoes. More specifically, Kinney's Shoes. Wherever a Kinney's Shoes was opening, there was a good chance he'd build a Shakey's next to it. I never would have thought that beer, pizza, and loafers matched well with ragtime music, but then again, I never got rich off of making making pizza franchises, either.

Business grew throughout the rest of the `50s and well into the `60s too. When Shakey Johnson sold his share in the business to Colorado Mining in 1967 for $3 mil-

Totally Pizza

lion, Ye Public House for Pizza and Beer had 272 locations across the country. A year later, when Plummer sold his half to the company for $9 million, Shakey's opened its first international franchise in Winnipeg, Manitoba, Canada.

By 1975, the company was under new ownership by Hunt International and had expanded to the Philippines and Japan. Moreover, the restaurant chain had roughly 500 stores across the United States.   Now, there are still around 500 Shakey's locations—worldwide. There are currently more Shakey's restaurants in the Philippines than the United States. As of 2011, there were domestic 58 stores total, with 51 of them in California. Oh, that's not a typo. If you're pissed off that there's no Shakey's near you, consider blaming Inno-Pacific Holdings of Singapore. The company took ownership of Shakey's in 1989. In the 14 years they helmed the pizza chain, they cut off more joints than an orthopedic surgeon with a thing for "bath salts." Locations and royalties fell steadily. Inno-Pacific's pizza parlor killing spree ended when a group of franchisees banded together and took the parent company to court for $20 million alleging breach of contract, breach of the covenant of good faith and fair dealing, fraud, and negligent misrepresentation. Plaintiffs said that during Inno-Pacific's 14-year watch, the company diverted franchisee royalties to its other interests instead of using them to develop and grow Shakey's. It didn't help that Inno-Pacific hired and fired 12 Shakey's presidents between 1989 and 2002. The holding corporation sidestepped trial by settling, then sold Shakey's to Jacmar Companies of Alhambra, California (which owned 19 franchises prior to the purchase) for $4.5 million in 2004.

Like Shakey's, Disney sent a lot of its operations to Asia in the 1980s and 1990s—partly to promote the brand like the pizza chain did (via Tokyo Disneyland) and partly as a coldblooded way to screw American animators (via outsourcing jobs to save cash). Both ventures worked out better for the Mouse, though.

All That Jazz

Remember when people used to sit around and listen to the radio for fun, just like TV? Yeah, neither do I. When Shakey's opened in 1954, though, that's precisely how the owners got the word out. Initially, Shakey's gained notoriety outside of its Sacramento home not for its pizza, but for the jazz program it sponsored on regional radio. In fact, Shakey Johnson did so much for ragtime jazz that the American Banjo Museum in Oklahoma City honored him with membership in its National Four String Banjo Hall of Fame for all the years he used banjo music at his pizza parlors. Sadly, the original employee uniforms have yet to enjoy the same honor at the National Celibacy Museum, but there's still hope.

Totally Pizza

Special Guest Star

For those who're familiar with the mysterious invention called "cable television," you may know Shakey's from South Park, where it's been featured more than once. The pizza chain got its big break in comedy on the episode "Kenny Dies" when Cartman uses stem cells to make his own Shakey's restaurant.

Ante Up

According to Technomic's Pizza Consumer Trend Report for 2012, 41% of the consumers they polled munch pizza once a week, as opposed to the 26% in 2010. The report says that new specialty pizzas, gourmet ingredients, and menu items that aren't pizza are driving up business. When the economy went into a coma in 2008, pizza chains responded with special offers and coupons that are still pulling in customers. Cheap, higher-quality frozen and take-and-bake pizza has helped too.

Pizza Hut: Resistance is Futile

"We looked very hard at Shakey's and asked ourselves if we wanted to be in the entertainment business. The answer was 'no.' We wanted to be a neighborhood pizza place." —Pizza Hut co-founder Frank Carney

Pizza Hut should be thankful there wasn't a Chippendale's in Wichita, Kansas back in 1958. Otherwise, founder Frank Carney might have opted to finance his college education through stripping. Instead, he and his co-founders started what would become the largest pizza franchise machine on the planet. Shakey's may have gone the franchise route first, but Pizza Hut paved the road and widened it. (Domino's perfected the car pool lane, but we'll talk about that later).

Frank was an electrical engineering major at the University of Wichita who, like his siblings, worked at the family grocery story. Their father had died at a young age, and the store was his legacy. Frank was nineteen when he finished his freshman year at college, and the beer joint next to Carney's Market threw in the bar towel. At a friend's suggestion to Frank's older brother Dan, the brothers decided to open a pizza place. Their business strategy at the time was "Ready. Fire. Aim." Neither of them knew anything about making pizza. True, they'd both dabbled in eating it, but flying a plane isn't the same as designing a fighter jet, now is it? That's where John Bender entered the picture.

Pizza Hut was founded by the Carney boys and Bender, with 600 bucks they borrowed from Mother Carney to start the business. Of the three, Bender was the only one with any pizza experience, unless you count the couple of times Dan ate pizza while serving in the Air Force. Bender was an Air Force pilot stationed nearby who'd worked in a pizza joint prior. He needed a part-time job and working with the Carney boys gave him that. He lived near one of the Carney sisters and had made pizza for her and her husband a few times in his apartment.

Some used pizza equipment and a signed lease later, they were in business. They just needed a name. While mom's loan had carried them this far, there wasn't

65

Totally Pizza

enough left to buy a new sign. The one they'd inherited from the beer bar had enough space for eight letters. Since "pizza" had to be four of them, that left enough for a space and three more. Legend has it Dan's wife thought the building looked rather hut-like, and the name stuck.

When Pizza Hut opened at 503 South Bluff in downtown, competition in Wichita was nonexistent. Pizza was a stranger—people knew of it, some had met it, but it most hadn't taken the time to get to know it. The owners introduced customers to pizza by giving it away on opening night. Pizza Hut originally sold a small pizza for $.95 and a large one for $1.50. Business boomed so much that six months later Bender and the Carneys opened a second location. Growth accelerated; when one of the managers wanted to open his own, the partners gave him the okay, provided he take it to Topeka. The Carneys wanted to keep all the Wichita stores for themselves. By the end of 1959 Pizza Hut was a corporation and manager Dick Hassur had that first Topeka franchise of his up and running.

A little over a hundred years after the California Gold Rush, the Kansas store was running on overdrive. Pizza Huts sprouted all over the Midwest in the early `60s like so many gold-laying geese. Most of those early franchises went to friends and employees who got the same deal Hassur did—pay Pizza Hut a fee to use the name in your designated territory, and they'd train you and let you use their recipes. Wich-

I know this looks like a quaint one-room schoolhouse, but it's actually the very first Pizza Hut building from Wichita, Kansas. Photo by Sanjay Acharya, CC BY-SA 3.0, via Wikimedia Commons

ita became the eye of a twister the likes of which Kansas had never seen before: one made of tomato sauce and cheese. The Pizza Hut tornado couldn't throw a pig ten miles, but you could certainly get it on your pie.

Five years after co-founding Pizza Hut, John Bender was bought out by the Carney brothers. By this time, Ma Carney was pretty sure her boys weren't going back to college any time soon. She wasn't exactly thrilled by the situation, but seeing how her sons almost had a license to print money, she could only get so mad. Men went to college back then to get ahead. You can't get much further ahead than 145 locations in eight years—unless you run a Mexican drug cartel.

Unlike Shakey Johnson, who focused on Kinney's Shoe Stores, the Carneys aimed their business machine at small and medium-sized towns. It made sense—the model worked like a charm in Wichita and Topeka. The company introduced pizza to places that might not otherwise have met it for years. Pizza Hut got so good at opening up shop that they were able to get one up and running from nothing at the Oklahoma State Fair in a mere five days. Demand was huge, but Frank and Dan's work ethic, entrepreneurial moxie, and natural talent for business were more than up to the challenge.

Pizza Hut in the 1960s was a businessman's wet dream married to a logistical nightmare. Having that many stores in 1966 meant 145 cash cows bringing in money. It also meant keeping the herd happy and healthy to keep costs down. To that end, the company opened a home office in Wichita that year to sheep dog operations. It also standardized its brand. The early franchises were a hodgepodge of different buildings, so the Carneys called in an architect to come up with a standard building design. Two big innovations made strong branding like this a must for any national restaurant chain.

Franchise food owes a lot of its success to the Interstate Highway System started by Eisenhower in the late 1950s. The highways made family road trips easier and longer. Franchise food was the same in Chicago, Los Angeles, or anywhere else on Route 66. They gave strangers in a strange land something familiar they could trust to taste just like it did back home. The large, colorful signs and famous logos were also easy to spot while driving. Moreover, since the system was made to facilitate national defense, you could move tons of traffic long distances at high speed. Taken in conjunction with America's train system, that made supplying a large restaurant chain possible. Without that sort of infrastructure bringing supply and demand together faster than ever before, there might not be such a thing as national restaurant chains. The need for a recognizable brand you could see from the freeway may have have caused Pizza Hut to standardize its restaurants and brand as much as any other factor.

Totally Pizza

One other new invention fueled the need for universal design: television, the You-Tube of the 1950s and `60s. Some critics hated the visual new medium but, ad men loved it. TV was theater of the mindless. You didn't have to think about how it looked. The cameras did it for you. All you had to do was sit back, enjoy your pizza with the family while watching this new Super Bowl thing and let the repetitive ads fire their images into your subconscious. For a food chain, having all of your locations look like the ones in your commercials attracted customers in droves. Most people embrace the familiar. TV commercials bred that familiarity for you and the kids. How many of us remember hearing or saying, "Mom! Dad! It's that place from TV! Let's eat *there*!"?

By 1968 Pizza Hut had over 300 locations in the United States and its first in Canada. As great as all this growth was, though, guiding it was like steering a comet with a bath salts habit. Franchise owners used accounting systems as varied as their personalities—it took eight months to merge them into one coherent system. Sales flattened, and profits fell to match. What the company needed was strong, long-term planning. They got it in the early `70s. Instead of relying on the stats in Pizza Hut's yearly reports to dictate strategy, Frank Carney laid out plans for the longer haul: "We about lost control of the operations. Then we figured out that we had to learn how to plan." Part of that meant taking a firm hand with suppliers. If you're a restaurant company and you want to control the cost of ingredients, try owning the companies that make them. Pizza Hut joined forces with Sunflower Food Processors to create Sunflower Beef, Inc. and acquired an 80% stake in Ready Italy, a frozen crust maker. They also expanded the menu with sandwiches.

Another turning point occurred when Pizza Hut went public in `72 with a listing on the New York Stock Exchange. and began growing at an unprecedented pace. At the end of 1972, Pizza Hut made its long-anticipated offer of 410,000 shares of common stock to the public. It also turned into the restaurant equivalent of the Borg. The company expanded by purchasing three restaurant divisions, a restaurant supply company, and a food and supplies distributor. Resistance was futile. At the same time Pizza Hut expanded its control over its suppliers, the company also went on the offensive marketing-wise. They launched local and national campaigns to really get the word out. Spending on local advertising alone increased from $942,000 in 1972 to $3.17 million in 1974.

But the biggest change in the early `70s came from Dan Carney. Fifteen years after he co-founded Pizza Hut, he was done. The constant traveling took him away from family far more often than he liked. In 1973, he left the company in brother Frank's ever-more-eager and capable hands. During his tenure as *el jefe*, Pizza Hut grew to epic proportions. He actively courted franchisees and expanded the com-

Totally Pizza

The iconic red pagoda roof that distinguished Pizza Huts across the nation. This hut is from Athens, Ohio. Photo by Ed! at English Wikipedia, CC BY-SA 3.0, via Wikimedia Commons

pany aggressively. Resistance was, in fact, practically futile. By 1977, Pizza Hut pulled in $436 million and had over 3400 locations across the globe.

That's where Pepsi comes in. This is when the foundation was laid for all of those hermaphroditic Pizza Hut/Taco Bell/KFC joints that sprouted up in food courts and Wal-Marts all over America. Pizza Hut merged with PepsiCo in 1977, becoming the latest earner in the soft drink giant's stable. Less than twenty years after he and his partners started Pizza Hut for 600 bucks, Frank Carney sold the company to Pepsi for $300 million. For those of you kids keeping score, that's five hundred thousand times the original investment. That's not too shabby for three guys who barely knew what pizza was to begin with. Frank Carney stayed on to helm Pizza Hut afterward but that didn't last too terribly long. He had his sights aimed at PepsiCo's top food operations job, which would've put him in charge of every restaurant holding in the corporate collective. When the corporation passed him over for an outsider, Frank struck out on his own. We'll talk more about that later.

Pizza Hut in the early to mid-1980s was a little like the title character in *Rocky III*. It was the champ at the end of the 1970s, but new blood chipped away at its supremacy like so many Clubber Langs. Pizza chains like Little Caesar's and Domino's, both children of the sixties, grew so big they changed market conditions and forced Pizza

Totally Pizza

Hut to change in order to keep up. Up to this point, Pizza Huts were sit-down pizzerias. The up-and-comers offered something Pizza Hut did not—speed.

Time is a valuable currency in any era, but in the business-as-warfare atmosphere of the 1980s, it was practically priceless. Remember, this was the decade that gave us power ties and had executives reading Sun Tzu's *Art of War* like it was their own personal corporate horoscope. This is also when Pizza Hut gave birth to its Personal Pan Pizza in 1983. They gave customers a five-minute guarantee that this single-serving pizzalet would arrive like a good hooker—fast and hot. It was their version of a quick, affordable pizza that was an ideal lunchtime meal. In 1986 Pizza Hut opened its 5,000th franchise unit in Dallas, Texas. That's also when the company began home delivery service, a nod to just how much the competition had upped its game and redrawn the pizza landscape. By the 1990s the delivery and carryout business had grown to account for roughly 25 percent of Pizza Hut's total sales.

In the early 1990s, drive-thru units were added to Pizza Huts for even more convenience. Eventually, with more and more people seeking food-on-the-go, Pizza Hut shifted away from the sit-down model with its video games, juke boxes, pitchers of beer, and welcoming ambiance. The pizza giant now is known for soulless pick-up-or-delivery closets that dot the American landscape. These Pizza Hut Express units first appeared in shopping malls, where reduced overhead allowed Pizza Hut to really take its Personal Pan Pizza into the cheap fast food market. Since that time, Pizza Hut has positioned Express units in school cafeterias, sports arenas, office buildings, and major airports. The company saw these nontraditional locations as the fastest-growing sector of its operations in the first half of the 1990s.

You can't really fault Pizza Hut for changing gears like that, though. Blame the fast food market. When 1994 hit, the pizza market was flaccid, partly because other fast food companies slashed prices to draw away customers. If you can't (or won't) lower your prices to match your competitors, you'd better damn sure offer consumers more bang for the extra buck. This was when Pizza Hut gave the world the carbfest known as the Stuffed Crust Pizza, then got celebrities to pimp it in a series of TV ads. One even featured Ringo Starr playing with The Monkees.

After 2000, Pizza Hut engaged phase two of its master plan to get rid of the old sit-down establishments in favor of the Expresses. A lot of the Red Roof "old guard" joints have either gone out of business or have been converted to Express units. I'm sad to see them go, but unless this book does really, really well, I'm not in any danger of becoming a majority stock holder in PepsiCo anytime in the near future.

Totally Pizza

The Roof is on Fire

With the Soviet Union collapsing like one of my carpentry projects in 1990, Pizza Hut saw dollar signs beyond the Iron Curtain. That's the year it opened its first restaurant in Moscow. If you think Hawaiian Pizza is weird, check out Pizza Hut's "Moskva." If you're a fish, chances are you or someone from your school (hell yeah, pun intended) may end up on one. It's a pie topped with sardines, tuna, mackerel, salmon, and onion, which the company says is a favorite at the Moscow Pizza Hut. Pizza Hut also says the Moscow location became Pizza Hut's highest-volume unit in the world. Other Huts just behind in total volume are in France, Hong Kong, Finland, and Britain. Hong Kong customers apparently dig corned beef and Canadian bacon on their Pizza Hut slices, while curry pizzas are big in Asia and Australia. And then there's that cheese-burger pizza monstrosity in England. I like to think of it as Pizza Hut's middle finger to McDonald's for making...

McPizza? Really? Seriously?

Yep. Ronald McDonald experimented with this idea as far back as the 1970s. Test markets in the U. S. and Canada were the lab rats for three variations. The first was a line of personal-sized pizzas in the late 1970s that were test-marketed in stores near interstate highways around Milwaukee and Madison, Wisconsin. Another version was like McDonald's fried apple pies, only with pizza stuffing. By '89, McD's was testing a 14-inch traditional-style pizza in Evansville, Indiana and nearby Owensboro. The company was serious enough that two years later, there were 500 test markets for the new product before Ronald

The need for McPizza's special requirements and equipment kept it from being served before 4 pm. They also contributed to its demise. Photo courtesy of McDonalds.fandom.com

Totally Pizza

pumped the brakes on the clown car and kept the project in a holding pattern. In Canada (c. 1992–1999), the McPizza started off as a family-sized offering that was brought out to the table by an employee and placed on a raised rack in the center of the table. Later it was scaled down to a personal-sized pizza. Ronald and company even offered home delivery to customers in some areas.

Obviously, Pizza Hut wasn't ecstatic about all of this. They handled it with the same dignity, self-security, and maturity you'd expect—from a three year-old. When McPizza came to test areas in Salt Lake City and Charleston in 1988, Pizza Hut shaved the price of its Personal Pan Pizzas in both markets down to 99 cents, to undercut McDonald's McPizzas by around 25 cents (Personal Pans back in the dinosaur era of leg warmers and mullets were priced somewhere between $1.69 and $2). The immaturity really took off with Pizza Hut's ad campaign at that time, though. The company ran a series of TV commercials saying how "McSilly" it would be to buy a McPizza instead of their product. The 30-second ads said Pizza Hut's products had six mouth-watering toppings while the other had "McTwo," that it had two layers of cheese while the other had "McOne," and Pizza Hut's dough was made fresh while McDonald's came "McFrozen." The brick-like frozen McPizza was then dropped onto the counter and the wrapping read, "Remove lid before cooking."

Pizza Hut need not have worried. McDonald's even went so far as investing big bucks in special ovens and wider drive-thru windows, but with all of the experimentation, special construction, and expensive marketing they just couldn't make it work. McDonald's floor plans were every bit as strict as Pizza Hut's. There wasn't enough space for the new ovens and converting production took more time and money than McDonald's was willing to invest. Like Elvis, though, some McPizza fans refused to accept their idol's death. McPizza lives on in some international markets—like India, as the apple-pie-styled Pizza McPuff.

Meeting of the Pies
When Pizza Hut offered its new Pan Pizza take on its pie in 1980, the obvious conclusion was that the idea was inspired by Chicago. That's truer than you know. Frank Carney got the notion while meeting with none other than Ike Sewell. The Pan Pizza was born as a result. It's still one of Pizza Hut's most popular offerings.

Pop Quiz
How much cheese does Pizza Hut go through each summer?
A. 300 million pounds
B. 100 million pounds

Totally Pizza

C. 250 million pounds

D. 175 million pounds

Answer: B. 100 million pounds. The company goes through 300 million pounds of cheese in a year. Pizza Hut purchases more than 3 percent of all cheese production in the United States, which requires a herd of about 170,000 dairy cows to produce it. The work leaves them udderly exhausted.

True or False: Pizza Hut was the first national pizza franchise to let customers order online in Spanish.

Answer: True. Pizza Hut started offering that service in 2010.

From Russia with Crust

In 1990, Pizza Hut invaded the former Soviet Union with pizza. It must have made an impression on the political leaders. According to Taylor Branch's interviews with Bill Clinton, Yeltsin almost caused an international incident in 1995 when the Secret Service caught the drunk world leader outside the White House trying to hail a cab in his underwear. He told them he was trying to go out for pizza.

Pizza Hut sign in Moscow, 1990 just before the store opened. Photo by GeorgeLouis, CC BY-SA 3.0, via Wikimedia Commons

Totally Pizza

2001: A Slice Odyssey

In 2000, Pizza Hut's logo boldly went where no chain food logo had gone before—the International Space Station. The company brand was painted on the side of a Proton rocket destined for the orbiting astronaut base. A year later, the company teamed up with Russian food scientists to create and deliver the first pizza to the station. Hopefully, the pilot remembered the napkins and crushed red pepper packets.

Station captain Yuri Usachev proudly displays the first chain pizza out of the gravity well. Photo courtesy of NASA, Public domain, via Wikimedia Commons

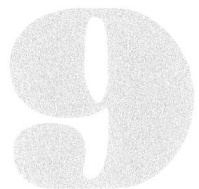

Domino's Domination
(in 30 Minutes or Less)

"He's very loyal to the people who work for him, but if he loses confidence in you for any reason, then it's like a light going off. Sometimes he's his own worst enemy."
— Anonymous Ave Maria University official speaking about his boss and Domno's Pizza founder, Tom Monaghan

Usually when you see that trait in a boss, it's right before the henchman who failed to kill Sean Connery is dropped into the shark pool. While Domino's Pizza founder, Tom Monaghan, isn't precisely a James Bond villain, he did build a worldwide organization and he does have a project in the works that some might call a secret lair. Before all of that, though, there was an orphanage—Saint Joseph Home for Children in Jackson, Michigan.

Tom and his brother James ended up there two years after their father's untimely death. Their mother had tremendous difficulty raising them so she placed them in the home until she was better able to give them the parenting they needed. Tom Monaghan was six when he went in, but by the time his mother collected her boys, he was twelve and the nuns' Catholic devotion rubbed off on him for the rest of his life. At one point, he even went to minor seminary in hopes of becoming a priest. A series of disciplinary infractions led to his expulsion, so he did what any red-blooded American kid would do: Monaghan enlisted in the United States Marine Corps. By accident. Yes, I know, military enlistment isn't like falling down a flight of stairs. The reality is that Tom thought he was talking to an army recruiter instead.

After finishing his tour in 1959, the 22-year-old Tom Monaghan pursued an architecture degree at the University of Michigan in Ann Arbor. It was 1960 when Tom and his brother (bought for the princely sum of $500) a pizza restaurant in Ypsilanti, Michigan named DomiNick's. A fifteen-minute pizza-making lesson from Dominick himself later, they were in business. Just like with Frank Carney, the plan was to use pizza profits to pay for college. At least, in Tom's case. Where Carney's busi-

Totally Pizza

ness exploded, though, the Monaghan brothers struggled. At first they ran the place in tandem while they learned the ropes. It was a small joint near Eastern Michigan University, which probably influenced Domino's franchising strategy later on. Eight months into the new venture, James made what might be the greatest trade blunder since the Czar sold Alaska to the United States in the 1800s: he traded his half of the company to Tom for a used Volkswagen Beetle. To his credit, how was he to know what the future held for the little pizza place? After all, it was losing money at the time.

Key changes in the 1960s turned that around. Instead of running his place like a Pizza Hut-style family operation, Tom Monaghan renamed the place Domino's and set his sights on a totally different group of pizzaphiles—college students. Perhaps his own experience as a student taught him the virtues of pizza as college sustenance. It was cheap, filling, tasty, and it was almost as great to eat cold the next day. What's more, you didn't have to know how to cook to get one. All of which are huge advantages over that other staple of university cuisine, ramen noodles.

Tom Monaghan also realized that pizza delivery was a mother lode waiting to be tapped. He just needed the right mining pick. Pizza makers tried everything to make their wares mobile since the early days in Naples—from vented copper pots back then to flimsy paperboard boxes in the mid-1950s, all of which fell short in the end. Tom solved the box problem, thanks to Triad Containers, a corrugated box company based in Detroit. In his autobiography, Monaghan said it was harder than he'd thought to design a box that folded easily while being strong enough to hold its shape while stacked. Triad helped him through the long process of coming up with

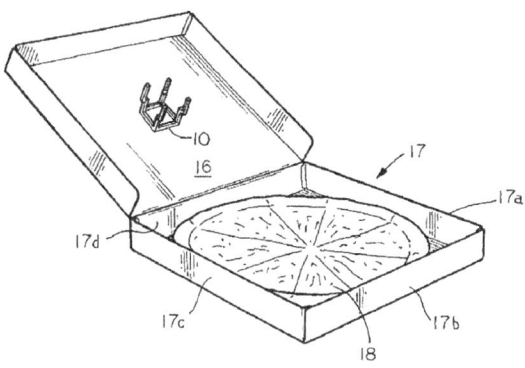

a cardboard box that was right for the job. Now that vented box is the industry standard for pizza delivery operations everywhere. Monaghan's only mistake was in not patenting the thing.

All of that took place in the early and mid-1960s. Shortly thereafter, Monaghan had his gold mine. In `65, he changed the business name to Domino's. Two years later, the

Tom Monaghan might have invented the pizza delivery box, but he didn't patent it. This image shows the invention of the nifty plastic spacer that keeps the lid from touching your cheese, invented by Ronald Drabick. Image courtesy US Patent Office

Totally Pizza

first Domino's Pizza franchise fired up its oven in Ypsilanti. Focusing on delivery gave Domino's a strong leg up during the late 1960s, especially when the East Lansing location gained massive popularity with car-less Michigan State University students craving convenient food. Business boomed enough to necessitate a logo—the idea was to add a new dot to it every time Domino's opened a new location. In 1969 there were three stores open, and with more of them on the way, Tom decided that three dots on the domino was plenty.

While Shakey Johnson opened locations wherever his Kinney Shoes fetish took him and Frank Carney focused on towns and small cities, Tom Monaghan set his locations near college campuses and military bases. All three chains had very different target demographics, yet each enjoyed success in the 1970s. Tom's business grew to 200 locations by 1978. Part of that was due to the infamous Thirty Minute guarantee. If your pizza didn't get there within half an hour of placing the order, it was free. That lasted until the mid-`80s when, it was reduced to $3 off. Between the late `60s and early `80s pizza delivery went viral (in the real world), largely in thanks to Domino's business model. There were obstacles along the way, of course, like the famous 1975 lawsuit by Amstar Corporation. It alleged trademark infringement and unfair competition (they owned Domino Sugar). That went away in 1980 when a federal appeals court found in favor of Domino's Pizza.

Domino's Pizza got much more interesting in the 1980s, too especially `83. Fifteen years after Pizza Hut went international, Domino's followed suit in May, 1983 in Winnipeg, Manitoba. With its 1000th location opening that same year, Domino's grew fatter and fatter. This was also the decade that saw the birth of The Noid, Domino's intentionally-annoying animated mascot.

Two more innovations brought Domino's into the limelight and kept them there. Making those magnetic car toppers for its delivery drivers was an act of marketing genius. The drivers were out making rounds anyway, so why not have their cars act as rolling billboards for the business? I don't think the company envisioned the idea being taken to taxicabs in Vegas advertising strip clubs, but that tells you just how successfully mobile advertising works.

And then there's the thermal bag. With other pizza hawkers running their own delivery services, Domino's had to keep quality a step ahead of the increasing competition. One invention that gave them an edge (for a time) was the thermal bag—the 1983 brainchild of Ingrid Kosar of Gilberts, Illinois. At least, she was the one who patented the idea. Vented cardboard boxes let hot, moist air out, which is great for crust consistency. Not so much for keeping a pizza hot, however. The soft, insulated bag retained the heat that escaped from the box, which kept delivery pizzas hotter for

Totally Pizza

longer. Domino's was the first to use it commercially, starting in 1984. Six years after that first Canadian Domino's and the 1000th location both opened up shop, Domino's number 5000 went into business. It wasn't a bad way to end the decade.

The 1990s, however, were more of a mixed bag. On the one hand, Domino's continued to grow, adding more locations all the time. But then Thirty Minutes or Less ran off the reservation, turned around, and tore a huge chunk out of the chain's ever-expanding financial ass. Not enough to make the company walk with a limp, but it certainly hurt. In 1992, Domino's settled a lawsuit at $2.8 million. It was brought by the family of a woman in Indiana who'd been killed by a Domino's delivery driver. When another woman who was injured by a Domino's driver running a red light was awarded almost $80 million in a 1993 lawsuit, that was enough for Tom Monaghan, who dropped the program later that year because of the "public perception of reckless driving and irresponsibility" regarding it. Incidentally, the injured lady was nice enough to accept $15 million instead of the full amount awarded to her.

The year 1998, though, was a good time to be Tom Monaghan. Thirty-eight years after he bought DomiNick's Pizza for $500, he sold 93% of the company to Bain Capital, Inc. for nearly $1 billion (with a "b") and stepped away from the chain's day-to-day operations. Six years later the company went public, with a Domino's employee ringing the opening bell the day its stock became available for purchase.

Faith Full

Tom Monaghan may have gotten the boot from seminary school, but he's always

kept his faith. While one hand helmed Domino's, the other wrote checks for and founded Republican Catholic institutions. Like the antagonist in a James Bond movie, he uses the proceeds from his business to further an agenda, only with the added bonus of communion wafers.

The church that pizza built: Ave Maria University in Florida.
Photo courtesy of Ave Maria University

Totally Pizza

In 1983 he established what is now the Ave Maria Foundation, to focus on Catholic charities, Catholic education, Catholic media, and community projects. Four years later, Monaghan helped form Legatus—an organization of Catholic business leaders. Its goal? To promote the ideals of the Catholic Church in society. He's also created Ave Maria Radio, the Ave Maria List pro-life political action committee, and the Thomas More Law Center—a public interest law firm dedicated to conservative issues such as opposing abortion, opposing same sex marriage, and opposing secularism.

In 1989, four years after he founded Ave Maria, NOW boycotted Domino's Pizza because Monaghan helped finance a referendum drive ending Medicaid-funded abortions in Michigan. Since Bain Capital bought him out in `98, Tom Monaghan has committed himself to spending his fortune on what he sees as philanthropic causes and endeavors. People may love or hate his views, but no one can dispute his work ethic or the role he played in making pizza delivery flourish around the globe.

Choir Boyz in the Hood

Early in 2002 Tom Monaghan tried to build Ave Maria University in Ann Arbor. More precisely at Domino's Farms, the huge corporate office complex he owned and leased to Domino's Pizza. His schematics included a 250-foot-tall crucifix. It didn't take an elite secret agent to thwart his master plan. Local officials refused to approve the zoning change that would've let him erect his pimpalicious bling.

You'd think that'd be the end of it, but no. Tom joined forces with local leaders in Collier County, Florida for a sequel. They offered him the ultimate sandbox to develop the university—a nice, big chunk of undeveloped land thirty miles east of Naples, Florida. Ultimately the university morphed into a city. Namely, Ave Maria, Florida.

Monaghan and his business partner, Barron Collier, broke ground on the project in February of 2006. Since they controlled all of the land in town, the guys decided to make whatever rules they wanted. In 2005, Monaghan had gone so far as to say that retailers in the "community" would be forbidden from selling contraceptives or pornography. I don't know about you, but denying a bunch of college students access to birth control or porn sounds like giving a chimp a rocket launcher to me. Fun to watch, but it usually doesn't end well for the chimp. Only in this case, the chimp ends up making a bunch of other chimps on accident. And you're not even rewarded with a fiery explosion.

The ACLU fired back with legal and moral criticism. Lawsuits clouded the horizon, sending Monaghan into damage control mode. He and the developers launched a public relations campaign to bury the idea that Catholic doctrine held the same authority as government law.

Totally Pizza

The Noid 1.0
Way back in 1986, before humanity was enslaved by computers, animators created cartoons by hand. Shocking, I know. That was the year famed clay animator Will Vinton breathed life into the putty blob known as The Noid. It was an advertising gimmick meant to be the avatar of crappy pizza service (getting annoyed, or "a noid"). Pons Maar voiced the critter in a series of ads for Domino's during the `80s. The commercials pimped the slogan, "Avoid the Noid."

With kids like me solidly addicted to computer games and pizza, Domino's branched out 1989 with a computer game dubbed Avoid the Noid for the Commodore 64 and MS-DOS home computers. You had to deliver a pizza within a half-hour time limit in an apartment building swarming with Noids, some of which packed heat. In 1990, Capcom released a different video game, Yo! Noid, for the NES.

ParaNoid
Kenneth Lamar Noid was a mentally ill Domino's customer who thought Domino's was targeting him with the Noid ads as a personal attack. On Januaray 30, 1989, he held two employees of an Atlanta, Georgia, Domino's restaurant hostage for over five hours. Like any other hostage taker, he had a list of demands for law enforcement. Some, like $100,000 and getaway transport were understandable Why he'd ask for a copy of The Widow's Son, though, is his own business (I'm pretty sure a hundred grand would have gotten him at least one copy). After forcing the hostages to make him a pizza, Noid surrendered to the authorities. Police Chief Reed Miller's assessment to the media of Kenneth's state-of-mind was one for the history books: "He's paranoid." Although Noid was charged with kidnapping, aggravated assault, extortion, and possession of a firearm during a crime, he was found not guilty by reason of insanity.

The Noid 2.0
In 2009, Domino's brought the Noid back from the dead—for a limited time only. This incarnation was made out of cotton instead of clay, in the form of "Avoid the Noid" t-shirts. Proceeds from the sales went to St. Jude's Children's Hospital. Don't feel left out if you didn't get one. The shirt run was limited to 1000. The Noid has had cameos on both Family Guy and twice on The Simpsons. The mascot's also been exploited on Facebook and had a 25th birthday video game made in its honor called "The Noid's Super Pizza Shootout."

Totally Pizza

Noid merch, courtesy of media.dominos.com

Sons of Glitches

When America's economy routed in 2008, Domino's planned a bailout of its own. The plan was to run a promotion code on the company website in December. They dropped the idea, which would have been fine...if someone had told their software programmer. The promotion code "bailout," never was deactivated. Sometime in early 2009, someone discovered the still-active code when they typed the word in as a promotion code. He or she posted the information online and 11,000 free medium pizzas later, the corporation figured out what was happening. It deactivated the promo code on March 31 of that year. Needless to say, the store owners on the business end were less than thrilled. Domino's promised to reimburse them for the lost pies.

Papa's Got a Brand New Bag

In 1998, Domino's upped the ante on pizza bag technology with its HeatWave thermal bag. Unlike the old version, it actually heats the pizza instead of just trapping the heat while it slowly dissipates. It's able to work this magic thanks to an electric heating element embedded inside. The element is made from a rubber-like phase-change material that's designed to stay hot after it's unplugged. It's a neat little device consisting of an electrical grid between two discs. When it's plugged in the grid heats the discs, which get hot enough to soften. Once unplugged, the discs get hard, giving off 170 degrees of steady heat.

Papa John's: This Means War

"They had become an assembly line product company. With PepsiCo, the drive for growth at almost all cost caused them to denigrate the product." —Pizza Hut founder and Papa John's franchise mogul Frank Carney, regarding Pizza Hut's quality at the 1999 Pizza Expo

In 1994, Papa John's scored a huge coup. They stole Frank Carney. Okay, maybe "stole" is a touch melodramatic. "Wooed" is far more accurate. Following his divorce from Pizza Hut in 1980, Carney, like many others leaving a long-term relationship gone bad, aimed his newfound freedom at playing the field—financially speaking. Instead of a six-month blur of one-night stands engaged in by the typical newly single, Frank Carney turned to the fiscal equivalent—venture capitalism. At first, he made a killing, nearly doubling his money in a few short years—but by 1989, his luck was flagging. When the recession hit in the early `90s, it stripped away his remaining gains like a gold digging lover with a hot body and a cold gambling habit. By 1993, the millions were gone. His biggest regret about that time wasn't for himself or the money, but for bringing his wife into that situation. In one interview, he said, "If it had been her fault, then I would have been okay with eating humble pie together. But it was my fault, and I caused her to eat it."

In the midst of Frank's investing adventures, young John Schnatter was learning the restaurant ropes, first with Rocky's Sub Pub in Jeffersonville, Indiana while going to high school, then throughout college at Ball State University, and finally at a tavern co-owned by his dad, with the cool name "Spaghetti's Lounge." Come 1984, he sold his 1971 Camaro Z28, used the funds to buy out the other half of the business, and thus launched what would become Papa John's, the third largest pizza chain in America. And Frank Carney was going to help him do it.

While Pizza Hut spent the 1980s expanding its product line with stuffed crusts, Personal Pan Pizzas, and Buffalo wings, Papa John's hugged a narrow focus—a sweet pizza sauce topped with fresh ingredients. Moreover, its locations were mainly

Totally Pizza

delivery and carryout operations from the get-go, whereas Pizza Hut had to restructure its restaurant model to fit changing customer preferences. And by having fewer options in crust styles and side dishes, Papa John's simplified inventory management. That let them keep their focus on quality.

Ten years after John Schnatter sold that Camaro, Papa John's was a publicly held company with 1000 stores when Martin Hart gave Carney a call. Hart used to sit on the Pizza Hut board, but he'd jumped ship to be a Papa John's franchisee in Houston. He told the Pizza Hut founder to check out a Papa John's store because it was right up Carney's alley, combining fast growth and quality pizza. Seeing was believing; Carney's visit sold him on the company. Once he took out a mortgage on the house to get a Papa John's franchise up and running, he was back to his forte: pizza, pizza, and more pizza.

At first, John Schnatter wasn't convinced, and who could blame him? Frank Carney franchising a Papa John's back then would be like Bill Gates opening a

string of Apple Stores now. When Martin Hart called John with the good news, he kept waiting for the punchline, even when Hart told him Carney was coming in for a sit-down. John Schnatter went from skeptic to student, expanding his pizza IQ while learning to trust his instincts and avoiding the trap of bureaucracy holding back operations and profits.

In 1997, Papa John's put Frank on camera in a TV ad. He announced to a mock group of Pizza Hut board members that he'd found a better pizza. Not only did that capitalize on his return to pizza, it multi-tasked as a 30-second middle finger to the company that passed Frank Carney over in 1980 and took his pride and joy away from the model he'd created. According to him, it wasn't

The car that built pizza: Papa John Schnatter poses with the 1971 Camaro he sold to start Papa John's. Image courtesy of Papa John's International, Inc.

payback—it was just a business opportunity that made sense. Pizza Hut execs were pissed, but it was their own fault. They essentially drove Yoda off their Jedi Council. Frank was less than sympathetic about their knotted panties, too. "All of those guys are worth millions now. If I'm taking bread off their tables, I'd like to know which condo or summer home they are talking about," he said to the *Houston Chronicle* in 1997.

Between that ad and others put forth by Papa John's touting their emphasis on quality, bad blood gushed all over the place—in the courtroom and on the street. Pizza Hut countered the ad campaign with a nice, fat lawsuit, alleging false claims in Papa John's commercials. When the case went to trial, the court agreed with Pizza Hut's argument that Papa John's slogan did not constitute statements of literal fact. The "fresher ingredients" in the ads didn't necessitate a better pizza in a restaurant. Appeals followed, of course. Eventually, the court ruled in favor of Papa John's in 2000. While the court upheld the jury's decision, it also said Pizza Hut failed to prove that the "misleading advertising" and puffery had a material effect on consumer purchasing decisions. That wasn't enough to make the two big kids play nice, however. A 1998 article in *Fortune* magazine summed it up with this observation from Gerry Durnell, the publisher of *Pizza Today* magazine: "It's like watching elephants mating. It doesn't happen very often, but when it does, it creates a lot of noise and stirs a lot of dirt. It's an awesome sight."

In 1999, Frank Carney was a feature speaker at the Pizza Expo in Las Vegas. He wasn't shy about telling the 900 or so franchise operators listening that he had no qualms or regrets about criticizing the company he co-created all those years ago. Frank felt free to do that because in his eyes Pizza Hut sold product beneath the standards established on his watch.

Nor was this pizza warfare confined to the generals. The *L.A. Times* ran an article that said Pizza Hut employees followed Papa John's drivers covertly so they could give Pizza Hut coupons to people who'd just ordered from the other company. Not to be outdone, Papa John's parked its trucks in front of Pizza Hut locations—and handed out free pizza to customers going into the place. At one point, Pizza Hut "gifted" franchisees with cheap toy punching bags with "Sock it to Papa John's" in big red letters on them. Rumor even has it that the Pizza Hut corporate jet had a Papa John's sticker in the toilet.

Today, Papa John's has over 3,400 restaurants in 50 states and 30 countries. About 133 are owned by Frank Carney and his business partner, Martin Hart.

"The Circle is Now Complete..."
Never underestimate the love for a good car. When John Schnatter sold his 1971

Totally Pizza

Camaro Z28 for $2,800 to buy the other half of what would be the family business back in 1983, you can bet he missed his sweet ride—maybe a little too much. Like any creepy old boyfriend on Facebook, he stalked the four-wheeled love of his youth later in life. On August 26, 2009, he repurchased his old love for $250,000. In celebration, Papa John's offered a free pizza to anyone who owned a Camaro.

Autocrats

John Schnatter isn't the only pizza exec with the sport car bug, either. In 1986, Tom Monaghan owned one of only six Bugatiti Royales in the world (for which he paid a mere $8.1 million). Frank Carney wasn't immune either. He and two other drivers on his racing team drove their Porsche 911 to fourth overall and victory in its class at the 24 Hours of Daytona in 1977.

"I Like it When They Call Me Big Papa..."

Nothing in the names Robert Graham, or John Schnatter says, "Papa." This faux familial affectation is how marketing execs try to fool us into thinking of corporate pizza as modest, familial, and homey, as if it was conceived in some old Italian immigrant's kitchen somewhere. When you make your pizza in a frozen food factory or design it in a boardroom, the last thing you want is too much honesty in the name. No one wants to buy a pie from "Focus Group Pizza."

Trump Card

Domino's hasn't been immune either. In 2005, Domino's supposedly paid $2 to $4 million to feature in an episode of the NBC reality series, *The Apprentice*. Contestants had to create and market their own pizza. What was supposed to be huge product placement to raise Domino's diminishing profits didn't work out that way—courtesy of Papa John's. An errant press release made its way to the rival's corporate HQ and John Schnatter gobbled up all the show's commercial airtime that he could. His ads carpet-bombed *The Apprentice* viewers with the line, "Why eat pizza made by apprentices when you can call the pros at Papa John's?"

Flame Wars

Most business owners (and online trolls) have enough sense to confine their flame wars to burning each other in online forums. Not in Florida, though. In October 2011, two managers at a Lake City Domino's were arrested for torching a Papa John's in the same town. One of them confessed to the crime, the other was caught soon after. The motive? Increased business if the Papa John's was out of business. The two men also rigged an ignition device out of an eight-inch-long clock, a 9 volt battery, enough black powder to fill a golf ball, and a plastic bag.

It's Not the Size of Your Pizza, It's How You Use It

In 2007, news.com.au ran a story about pizza shrinkage Down Under. Not the kind a man experiences when he gets into the pool—although you wouldn't have thought that from the YouTube video. Yes, a major pizza chain in Australia produced a video suggesting a rival's drivers were a little light in the penis department.

Eagle Boys Pizza made the video, which inferred the shortcoming in Domino's drivers. Not only did the company run it on YouTube, it also ran the short on its website. The video parodied a government safety ad that shows women waving their pinkies at speeding drivers. Part of clip's purpose was to point out the fact that Domino's reduced the size of its pies in response to Pizza Hut doing the exact same thing. Domino's defended the action by saying it was necessary to remain competitive in the market.

At the time, Eagle Boys marketing manager Scott Hamilton said: "Multinationals like Domino's Pizza are selling smaller pizzas than Eagle Boys and expected customers not to notice. It's disgraceful and frankly un-Australian." Needless to say, Domino's wasn't too happy about the whole incident.

Personally, I'd insert some "Thirty Minutes or Less" innuendo to make the wound extra salty, but that's just me. Not that I have anything against Domino's. I just think being a smart ass should be savored like fine wine (or great pizza).

Oh, Who are the People in Your Neighborhood...

In the 1990s, Louisville was home to both David Novak, the president of Pizza Hut's parent company, Tricon, and Papa John's founder John Schnatter. If you think seeing your ex at the supermarket is uncomfy, imagine living down the street from them while they are insulting you on public television and trying to take your money. "Awkward" isn't a big enough word to cover that, and it's seven letters long. Both lived in a small suburb east of town named Anchorage. Their kids went to the same school, they kicked in money to rebuild the same church, and they even played in the same golf trio. Novak claimed he was above the petty jabs at Papa John's, but Schnatter was supposedly more direct, allegedly saying that while he liked Novak, he didn't respect him.

Local people were quick to start all kinds of rumors about the warring execs. One held that (insert name here) tried to bribe the pastor with a house if he'd kick (insert other name here) out of the congregation. Another said that local food photographers were forbidden from shooting Papa John's pizzas if they'd ever taken a photo of a Pizza Hut pie. The truth of this soap opera can't be verified, but Anchorage residents definitely took an interest in the Pizza Wars.

When Schnatter and his company gave the University of Louisville $5 million to help build the new Papa John's Cardinal Stadium, not only did Novak decline Schnatter's invitation to the opening game, Pizza Hut began airing a commercial depicting Papa John's employees pouring soaking, canned mushrooms onto a pizza.

Papa John's Vs. ...Racoon Ass?

In August of 2012, Stephen Colbert had this to say after hearing reports that Papa John's CEO John Schnatter told investors that "Obamacare" would force the company to raise the prices of its pizza in 2014 by 11 to 14 cents: "People will not pay another cent because when you order a Papa John's pizza, it's only after you've reached a state of such desperate gnawing hunger that you'd eat the ass off a raccoon that drowned in your bird bath, and, even then, only after making absolutely sure that you're all out of drowned raccoon ass," he added. "And now Obama expects you to shell out almost three extra nickels for this hot turd pie? F@%* that! Eat the nickels, you have your dignity." Snap!

11 Chuck E. Cheese: Welcome to Fight Club

"The biggest problem is you have a bunch of adults acting like juveniles. There's a biker bar down the street, and we rarely get calls there." —Brookfield, WI Police Captain Timothy Imler, about the mass melee at a local Chuck E. Cheese

When I heard about Chuck E. Cheese's Pizza Time Theatre as a kid, I didn't believe it. No one makes a pizza place with cartoon characters, video games, skeeball, and an all-you-can-eat sundae bar. That would be like making a pocket phone that lets you watch TV, or drafting the best players in the NBA for the men's Olympic basketball team. Things like that are just too perfect to happen. Yet, that's exactly what went down in 1977. It was the year Nolan Bushnell re-invigorated the entertainment pizza sub-genre with what is now Chuck E. Cheese's. While Pepsi was buying Pizza Hut, Atari was founding Pizza Time Theatre. At least, Atari's boss man was. A few years prior to his venture into pizza, Bushnell created Pong, then started (and ran) Atari.

So why is Chuck's so special? Because it combines Disneyland, birthday parties, video games, gambling, and beer. It's what Disneyland would be like if Bugsy Siegel was Walt's co-creator. Flash back to the early or mid-1970s and you'll find kids pouring their allowances into the newfangled joystick bandits called "video games" faster than Granny's social security check at a slot machine. The big difference being that every once in awhile the slots actually spit money back at you. Children weren't alone, either. Bowling alleys, pizza parlors, and even bars started carrying the latest coin-op games. Eventually, there were full-blown video arcades with nothing but games, a few change machines, and a surly cashier whose job it was to make sure the machines didn't get broken into.

Many of those games came from Bushnell's Atari. Nolan understood their appeal better than most people think, though. In 1968, he graduated from the University of Utah College of Engineering with a degree in electrical engineering. If you've ever heard of a computer game called *Spacewar!*, you know it was one of the first com-

Totally Pizza

puter games in the world. The university was big into computer graphics research, so they were heavily involved with the game.

When Bushnell finished his degree, he and Ted Dabney Yyed while trying to market a stand alone *SpaceWar!* Clone in arcade game form. In order to keep the lights on at the new company, they took on a route servicing pinball machines while the two men made the prototype. This wasn't Nolan Bushnell's first encounter with amusement park games, either. He'd worked for Lagoon Amusement Park in Ogden, Utah while a high school lad. Carnival games were of great interest to him—especially those where suckers, er, customers pitted luck and skill against the odds to win a prize. If you think the stuffed animals at the circus were overvalued in relation to how much it took to win one, computer games were worse. After spending countless hours and quarters mastering them, all you had to show for it was a high score, which usually disappeared when the power shut off and reset the next day when the arcade opened. Nolan's passion for games and theme parks led to the launch of Atari, Chuck E. Cheese's Pizza Time Theatre, and later on, a social staple of `80s teenage life: pizza and home video games.

By 1977, Atari was a huge success—so much so that Warner Communications bought it from Nolan Bushnell for a cool $28 million. Bushnell's experience in the

Chuck poses with one of his worshipful acolytes. Photo by Arcade Heaven via Flickr

Totally Pizza

amusement park industry and his love of Walt Disney's work were huge influences on the Pizza Time Theatre concept. In fact, Nolan applied for work at Disney more than once after graduating from college, only to be turned down each time. Just like the first Shakey's, the first Pizza Time Theatre opened up in Northern California, although it was in San Jose instead of Sacramento. In November 1978, Bushnell left Atari to purchase the Pizza Time Theatre concept from Warner Communications.

The idea was to marry video arcades, animatronic characters, arcade games, and pizza in one big family. Unlike a Shakey's or other pizza parlor, Chuck E. Cheese's focuses almost entirely on the kids. Not coincidentally, the chain served as the perfect distribution tool for Atari arcade games. There really isn't much there for an adult unless you're the creepy sort with a panel van and a bunch of free candy. In fact, since its founding, Chuck E. Cheese has gotten a reputation for pizza that takes a back seat to entertainment in the quality department.

If you're an adult, a Chuck E. Cheese party may feel more like a tour of duty in Vietnam. The conflict begins with the parents. Wandering the restaurant like so many LBJs and Westmorelands, these poor souls are the architects of the Chuck E. party fiasco. They've invested a lot of time and money into a situation they no longer control and that no longer makes sense. Sure, it all started innocently enough, but when will it be over and how much will they have to commit before they can pull out?

Then there are the pawns in this conflict, the kids. No amount of pre-school or Schoolhouse Rock can prepare them for this electronic jungle of lights and sounds, where mascots await around every corner to ambush the unwary. The green recruits have it pretty hard, facing the indirect fire of skeeball or tunnel ratting it in the slide complex. "Where do I commit my tokens so they'll do me the most good?" they wonder. Many begin drinking soda to escape the harsh reality of the situation in a sugar-induced high. But the veteran kids may have it worse. These are the children with the thousand-yard stare who've seen the elephant, and it's now a part of them forever. For them, they're not at a birthday party, they're "in country." You can spot the vets in the field at skeeball shouting, "Git some!" Once they're back in the world, they'll never be the same.

But it's the workers at Chuck E. Cheese who are the real victims. These poor innocents seek to go about their daily business amid this horrid chaotic background. It's not uncommon for the workers to catch some stray soda or pepperoni shrapnel between groups of unruly toddlers. But they endure, patiently awaiting a time when the party will be over, and they can go back to a normal life of high school.

When the end does come, it takes the form of a minivan sent from The World. The parents have depleted all of the resources set aside and are forced to evac their troops from the conflict before it gets any worse. Tired, they finally head for home.

Eventually, Nolan Bushnell left Chuck E. Cheese to pursue his other many ventures in computer gaming, with varying degrees of success. Lately he's been involved with Anti-Aging Games, LLC. On April 19, 2010 Atari announced that Nolan Bushnell was joining the company's Board of Directors. Chuck E. Cheese's has been through its ups and downs too, making changes to suit demand. When consumer interest in arcade games faded to the shadows, Chuck E. Cheese toned down their presence in many of its locations. You'll still find them there, just fewer in number.

Where a Kid Can be a Kid. And Dad Can be a Total Asshat

Personally, I don't go to Chuck E. Cheese looking for fights. That's what strip clubs are for. I don't really think most people go there looking to throw down, either. Regardless, fights break out often enough for ABC News' *Nightline* to have run a story on it in March of 2012.

You can see a lot of these fisticuffs on YouTube since someone usually has a cell phone camera handy to record the touching family moment for posterity. Seeing as how you have cheap beer, kids amped up on soda, and loud noise—all in a confined area with everyone trying to share time on a bunch of games—it's easy to see how matters can grow out of hand.

How bad does it get? One location in Pennsylvania called the cops to break up fights 17 times in 18 months starting in 2009. Not to be outdone, a Chuck E. Cheese in Brookfield, WI has called the cops 81 times since the beginning of 2007, according to the town police. Sometimes the brawls snowball until as many as 15-40 adults are going at it.

Some locations approach the problem with hired security, some of whom actually carry guns. A south Milwaukee location had 18 fights in two months, with one growing to 40 combatants. The neighbors and cops were less than thrilled by that, so the company addressed the problem by voluntarily giving up the store's liquor license. It was that or face closure. The situation got a lot better afterward, but it's debatable how much booze contributed to the problem. Adding armed guards and upgrading the parking lot lighting may have helped just as much, depending on who you ask.

To be fair, incidents like these are very rare relative to the number of guests that visit Chuck E. Cheese restaurants every year. According to a press release the company gave to *Nightline*, "For over 35 years, Chuck E. Cheese's has been providing a wholesome and safe environment for entertainment and meal occasions for families with young children. In 2011, over 99.99% of approximately 65,000,000 guest visits at Chuck E. Cheese's occurred without incident."

Totally Pizza

No Child Left Behind... Usually

In March of 2012, ABC News reported that there were five different incidents in recent years of kids getting left behind at Chuck E. Cheese restaurants. In one incident, a three year old was left behind *after her own party* at a location in Bel Air, Maryland. The parents paid cash, so the restaurant had no means to contact them. The family didn't even know she was missing until they saw her picture on the local news.

A second incident was even worse. In Pearland, Texas, Chuck E. Cheese employees noticed a five year old girl playing games all by her lonesome—at 10:30 at night. Child Protective Services stepped in and got the little girl back to her nearly hysterical mother, who was relieved to have her baby back. What most of these cases have in common is too many kids, not enough adults to sheep dog them all. I suppose it's also possible some of these children were left behind on purpose to give mommy and daddy a little extra quiet time. When you have a family with ten kids, one less rotter screaming at you for a few hours is probably a welcome blessing.

Chuck E. Cheese is a big f-ing rat. Here he is pre-2012 with baseball cap. Photo by downing.amanda, CC BY 2.0, via Wikimedia Commons

Extreme Makeover: Cartoon Edition

Let's get one thing straight. Chuck E. Cheese is a rat. No, seriously. The gray character is not a mouse, as some believe. Either way he looks pretty spry for a rodent over 35. His looks have changed through the decades. First with his bowler hat, then the baseball cap, and now the slimmer rock n' roll version the company rolled out in 2012. Duncan Brannan voiced the character starting in 1993 and after two decades of working for the company, he found out he'd been replaced when he discovered "Chuck's Hot New Single" video online. The company released a statement saying

Totally Pizza

that Duncan hadn't been fired but that CEC "chose to utilize a new voice talent." Now who's the rat?

Coin of the Realm

Like the gray rodent who pimps its pizza, Chuck E. Cheese's brass tokens have worn many faces over the decades. Numerous varieties exist and are collected by exonumia geeks (exonumia is a catchall for tokens, coins, medals; not a blotchy skin condition—I thought that when I heard it too). So, mom, if you're reading this, don't throw out those old tokens I left with my *Star Wars* toys. We may be able to get poker money for them on Ebay. Recently, the company started testing refillable cards with a magnetic strip to replace both the tokens you put into the game and the tickets you win for playing it. That's not nearly as satisfying as walking around with a fat wad of game tickets after conquering skeeball like it was France, but it reduces the need for paper products, and that's probably a good thing.

Think Different

Back when Nolan Bushnell ran Atari, two guys who'd helped develop the game Breakout cobbled together a device from borrowed Atari components. When they offered it to Bushnell, he turned it down because Atari's focus was on home gaming consoles and arcade games. Had he known what the two guys, Steve Jobs and Steve Wozniak, were going to do with their little "personal computer" invention, he might have reconsidered.

Chuck E. Cheese's token. Photo by outletpro from Winter Springs, USA, CC BY 2.0, via Wikimedia Commons

Frozen and Kit Pizza: Please Try This at Home!

"...they were cheap and children liked them. So did parents, especially since they didn't have to eat them." —Writer Curt Wohleber, describing frozen pizza in *Invention & Technology* magazine, 2005

Don't let the rise of civilization fool you. Humans are lazy. A lot of people only work as hard as it takes to get them what they need and want. If we all loved suffering, we'd still be chasing animals over cliffs every day instead of calling out for pizza or throwing a frozen one into the oven for thirty minutes. People have worked pretty damn hard to make life easier since Og decided it was simpler to divert water from the river to the grassland than hauling water by hand. Sure, there was the initial phase of work while you dug the ditch, but once that was done, you could see some use for this newfangled "farming" fad the kids liked.

Fast forward a couple of ice ages. Og's distant descendant risks a little carpal tunnel syndrome every time he/she orders a pizza online from the delivery joint nearby, then has to wait an agonizing half hour for it to get there, walk an entire 20 feet to the door, greet the delivery person, pay them, and include a tip. Oh, the horror.

For those unfortunates for whom this is simply too much of an ordeal, there's frozen or kit pizza. You still have the inconvenience of reading simple directions on the box, pressing the buttons on the oven, and waiting 20-30 minutes for your food, but no one ever said life was easy. And you don't have to tip.

With American prosperity in overdrive after World War II, middle class growth kept pace. People pounced on any new innovation that offered to make life easier, no matter how questionable. Remember, this was the time when school films promised us all flying cars and moon bases by the year 2000 or so—right after we all beat Communist Russia while practicing proper hygiene and abstinence, of course. Not only did this hunger for modern convenience in the 1940s and 1950s drive the push for pizzerias, it also gave birth to "do-it-yourself" pizza in the form of frozen pies or scratch-built pizza baked from kits found in the grocery store. Such conve-

Totally Pizza

nience "cuisine" spawned meals like the TV dinner, the instant pancake, and frozen fish sticks. As more and more ethnic foods emerged into the mainstream out of Little Italy and Chinatown, it was only a matter of time before some enterprising businessman applied freezer technology to a pizza or broke the ingredients down to fit the "just-add-water" mentality.

Roman Pizza Mix was the first company to make a DIY pizza kit back in 1948. Chef Boyardee followed suit with its pizza kit shortly thereafter, which you can still buy in the store today. For a lot of Americans, these home kits and their frozen cousins became childhood favorites. Most contain a bag of dry dough mix, a pouch (or can) of tomato sauce, and some sort of cheese-like substance with which to top the finished product. If you're the sort of loose cannon who likes toppings on your pizza, though, you've got to buy those separately. That pretty well takes the "cheap" out of "cheap and easy."

Frozen pizza gets around that. If my freshman year in college taught me one thing, it's that freezing food prevents rotting a lot better than sticking it in a cardboard box. Frozen pizza makers have a lot more leeway when it comes to variety than their kit pizza counterparts.

While kit pizza hasn't changed very much since its inception, modern freezer pie resembles its predecessor about as much as *Harry Potter* looks like *The Wizard of Oz*. When Celentano Brothers created the first mass-marketed frozen pizza in 1957, it wasn't even in the same league as what you'd get in a good pizzeria. For starters, early frozen pizza crust had all the backbone of a politician in an election year. Mostly this was because the ice crystals in the crust broke down its gluten. The toppings increased the problem. When heated, they released their moisture into the dough. Eating an early frozen pizza was akin to munching on watered bread topped with beef jerky. Fortunately, enough people liked frozen pizza to keep the business going strong. Other companies like Totino's and Tombstone tried their hand at frozen pizza over the years, experimenting with different ways to make the product work better.

Totino's Italian Kitchen was originally a pizzeria serving takeout when Rose and Jim Totino opened it in Minneapolis in 1951. They later turned it into a dine-in place when customers wanted to actually sit down and enjoy their pizza on-site. A decade later they had the idea to sell frozen pies that customers could bake at home. Seeing as how they were in Minneapolis, I'm guessing that keeping pizza cold on the way home probably wasn't an issue. By 1962 the product proved popular enough that they started Totino's Finer Foods and began mass production of frozen pizzas. The product's popularity skyrocketed, and by the early 1970s it was one of the most

Totally Pizza

popular frozen pizzas in America.

Frozen pizza was still a far cry from the fresh-baked version you smelled in a good pizzeria...at least, until 1979. That's when Rose patented a dough designed specifically for freezing. Originally, Totino's bought frozen dough from a plant in Chicago, brought it out to Minneapolis, and added the toppings in-house. Since Rose described the dough as "the industry standard cardboard crust," she probably wasn't a fan of it.

Demand still grew. Come 1971, business was so good that Totino's

Rose Totino, the mother of modern frozen pizza crust. This is an ad from 1986, courtesy of General Mills

constructed a $2.5 million production plant in Fridley. Two expansions later, they still couldn't keep up with consumer demand. What's more, Jim's health took a wrong turn. These two factors eventually lead the couple to sell Totino's Finer Foods to Pillsbury in 1975 for $22 million. Rose then became Pillsbury's first female corporate vice president, making it her personal crusade to solve the cardboard crust problem. Even with Pillsbury's considerable resources at her command, freezing the crust so it would stay crisp was a bit like chasing the God Particle with a kaleidoscope.

Eventually, they resorted to an old family remedy—frying. When Rose was a kid, her mother would fry the pizza crust when she made them for the family. So Rose and her team tried frying the dough instead of pre-baking it before freezing. The result was delamination-resistant pizza crust. That's a fancy way of saying it resisted the harsh ordeal of freezing and thawing much better than before. In 1979, she was even rewarded a patent for it.

Totally Pizza

Right around the time Totino's Finer Foods started making its pies *en masse*, Pep and Ron Simek ran the Tombstone Tap tavern one state over in Medford, Wisconsin. The place drew its name not from any morbid fetish of its owners but from the fact that it was next to a cemetery. One night, Pep, the showman of the two, decided a beer-soaked floor was the perfect place to demonstrate his mad dancing skills. Specifically, dancing the Peppermint Twist on the jukebox.

Pep's superstar moment ended with him on the floor and his leg in an odd position—the kind of odd that requires x-rays and a cast. Cursed with immobility and blessed by plenty of time to think, Pep used his long winter recovery playing in the 6 foot by 6 foot kitchen in the back (Ron's family lived in the back of the tavern too; the kitchen was also their personal cooking facility). Pizza was his Guinea pig of choice. The successful experiments he limped out to tavern customers. The failed ones...well, if I had to guess, I'd say he probably made use of the graveyard next door. I could be wrong, but any zombies rising from that place might be looking for pizza instead of brains. Thanks for the public service, Pep.

The genius marketers at Tombstone Pizza declared it to be the Official Pizza of Halloween. Then they designed several Halloween-themed labels to prove it. Photo by Mike Mozart via Flickr

Totally Pizza

The five-spice version he liked most drew customers like flies to, well, a corpse. Business took off so fast that their wives got into the act. The two couples started making extra pies, freezing them, and selling them to other local bars. Demand grew so much they had to buy a freezer truck capable of carrying 1800 pies. Even that wasn't enough. In 1970, eight years after Pep Shimek cut a rug and broke a gam, he and Ron broke ground on a factory in a large local industrial park to keep pace with all those beer-guzzling Wisconsin folks and their need for Tombstone Pizza. Beer drinkers weren't alone. Tombstone added bowling alleys, gas stations, and indie grocery stores to its clientele. By the time they sold the company to Kraft Foods in 1986, Tombstone Pizza was pulling in $100 million a year. Success stories like these were repeated all through the frozen pizza universe—start small, get big, sell the place to a large food corporation. Nestle, Quaker Oats, Kraft, and Pillsbury have all put their greedy fingers in the frozen pizza pie.

Even though frozen pizza (and all of its pizza-like brethren such as pizza rolls) had come pretty far since the 1950s, it was still franchise pizzeria's bitch as far as quality during the 1980s. In 1995, Kraft dropped a nuke that seriously narrowed the gap: DiGiorno. For years, Kraft's research division worked on a top secret project to make a frozen pizza with a self-rising crust like the hand-tossed pizza joint version. Add in DiGiorno's the emphasis on quality toppings instead of cheap ones—and the resulting superior pie—reset the standard for what could be done with frozen pizza. In the nearly 20 years since then, frozen pizza has continued to evolve, with makers offering not just different styles, but also gluten-free options and organic versions.

In the middle of all this, some pizza making mad scientists gene-spliced frozen and pizzeria pie, leading to the mutant hybrid known as "take-and-bake" pizza. It's like crossbreeding a vampire with a zombie, only tastier—all the strengths of its parents, none of the weaknesses. Take-and-bakes come fully assembled with toppings, like a frozen pizza. They're just made fresh in the supermarket or at specialist pizzerias like Papa Murphy's and Mom's Bake at Home Pizza. Consumers are not limited to whatever toppings some corporation decided they should have on their Tombstone—take-n-bake pizzas come as custom jobs. For a moderate fee, of course.

For a genetic mutant, take-and-bike pizza looks great for its age. Some people think it was born in the mid-1990s but it's at least 30 years old. No one knows precisely when it hit the market, but Mom's Bake at Home started selling them in 1981. From 1961 to 1980, Mom's founder Nick Castellucci sold hot pizza just like any other take-out pizza joint in Philadelphia. He also piled the toppings high for the fresh ones he brought home, then baked for his family. That led him to offering the same type of fresh, uncooked pizza to his customers. Nick may have sired the mutant, but Robert

Totally Pizza

Graham made it rampage. Graham launched fresh pizza from the last place you'd expect to find it—a convenience store.* One of his vendors carried a fresh, unfrozen pizza product. Robert knew home ovens didn't reach the 600 degrees F. needed to properly cook a pizzeria pizza, so he asked the guy how he made the crust. The man was all to happy to answer, provided Robert cough up $10,000 for the recipe.

Graham figured he could research it on his own and keep that ten grand in his pocket. About 250 recipes later, he had a dough that baked at 425 degrees F. in a home kitchen oven. With the money he saved, Robert Graham secured $100,000 in financing, then opened several Murphy's Pizza outlets in 1984. The results were pretty bad. While Graham had business experience, he didn't know thing one about running a restaurant. In 1988 he met Terry Collins, a longtime fast-food executive with experience at Burger Chef and Pepsico, who saw potential for the take-and-bake pizza concept. Collins bought 51 percent interest in the seven-store Murphy's Pizza chain for $500,000. His knowledge turned the business around. In 1990 Collins bought the 65-store Papa Aldo's chain for $1 million. Aldo's and Murphy's were a great fit. Aldo's had strong management but suffered from a crappy product. Murphy's had the opposite problem. Like take-n-bake pizza itself, the merger solved the problems of both parents. The two chains remained independent entities until 1995, when Collins merged them as Papa Murphy's International, Inc. Take-n-bake pizza proved so popular that Papa Murphy's was America's sixth largest pizza chain by the year 2000, when it hit the 600 locations mark. Other take-n-bake pizza businesses have sprung up all over the world.

Just like the name says, you pick up the uncooked fresh pizza from the shop, bring it home, and bake it in your oven whenever you want. Take-and-bake pizzas are typically made to order, although the pizzeria may also feature a number of its own recipe pizzas on hand for pick-up as well.

For pizzerias, offering take-and-bake has advantages. Costs tend to be lower than with a conventional pizza joint because you don't need ovens since you're not actually baking the pizza. That means lower energy costs, less restaurant space needed to run a take-and-bake pizzeria, and less staff (since you're not cooking or delivering the product.) Often times this enables them to undercut national franchises operating in the area.

Some take-and-bake shops are stand-alone operations like Papa Murphy's; others are part of grocery stores or delicatessens. National supermarket chains also offer their own take-and-bake pizza. It's gotten so popular even traditional dine-in pizza joints like Pizzeria Uno now offer it in some stores.

*Unless, of course, you really believe the cardboard-like bread slab with one

Totally Pizza

sausage nugget on it under a minimart heat lamp is good pizza. If so, please stop living under a rock. Life has more to offer.

Is It a Pizza or an Egg Roll? Tell it to Make Up its Mind and Come Back Later

There really was a Jeno behind Jeno's Pizza Rolls. His full name was Jeno F. Paulucci, and in his lifetime he started more than 70 companies—including Michelina's, Chun King, and of course, Jeno's Pizza Rolls.

Paulucci was born in the mining town of Aurora, Minnesota. The Pauluccis had moved to Minnesota from Italy and Jeno's dad Ettore worked the mine, but the family also

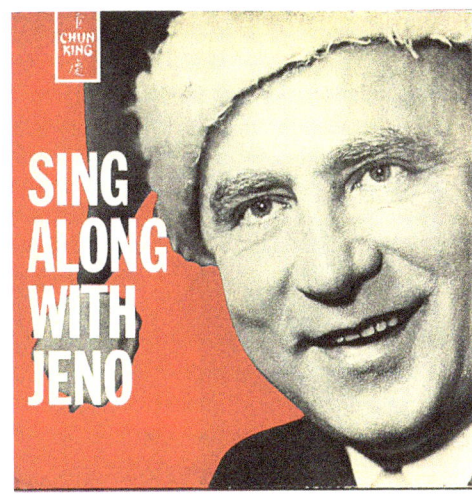

This fantastic 1964 promotional package was a gift to dealers and friends of the company most noted for Chun King Chinese food. The records are actually lids that went on the frozen food containers! Courtesy of the Internet Museum of Flexi/Cardboard/Oddity Records. I am not making this shit up.

had a small grocery store during the Great Depression. That's where Jeno got started.

During the 1940s, Paulucci developed his line of Chun King canned Chinese food products. Yes, the most famous Chinese canned food in the United States was started by an Italian immigrant in Minnesota. Marco Polo must have laughed his ass off in his grave about that. By 1985, Paulucci had created one of the most bizarre and successful culinary love children in America—Jeno's Pizza Rolls. It must have been successful. Why else would Pillsbury have bought the company from him that year for $135 million? Jeno Paulucci later suffered from seller's remorse, though, stating, "I should've kept the pizza roll. It's something that'll damn near live forever." In the early 1990s, Paulucci returned to northeast Minnesota to launch Luigino's, Inc., a frozen food company specializing in Italian food marketed under the Michelina's brand, named after Paulucci's mother.

Although he was big into charity work and pro-union, Jeno's life had its share of controversy. In 1982, he moved 1200 jobs from the Jeno's Pizza plant in Minnesota to Ohio, which had offered Paulucci publicly-financed low-interest loans. In response to criticism for this, Paulucci told Minnesota Public Radio, "I'm a businessman, I'm not going to say 'oh gee, I'm a nice guy.'"

Totally Pizza

Free Range Pizza?

Not quite, but close. In March of 2012, Annie's launched the first-ever organic rising-crust frozen pizza. The frozen pizzas are available at Whole Foods Market nationwide in Uncured Pepperoni, Four Cheese,Supreme and Spinach & Mushroom varieties. And the veggies and meats are certified—organic for you purists out there.

Chef Boy-Ar-Dee

His company name may sound like an `80s rap act, but Chef Ettore Boiardi's long career saw not only the launch of his pizza kit, it also had him running the prep for the homecoming meal served by Woodrow Wilson at the White House for 2,000 returning World War I soldiers. When Adolf Hitler needed straightening out in the next war, Boiardi's company made millions of rations for American and Allied troops during the conflict. The War Department (Defense Department, to all of you who slept through history class) rewarded his efforts with a Gold Star Order of Excellence. He was also awarded the Order of Lenin by the Soviet Union for supplying its troops with rations during World War II (a fact the company kept to itself during the Cold War). You may know him better as the old guy on the label of his products or from his company TV ads.

New York Prison Ban on Frozen Foods

Early in the history of frozen food, the quality was so low that New York prisons banned it. New York state law also forbade the sale of slow-frozen food unless you had a sign out front proclaiming, "Frozen Food Sold Here" in letters at least 8 inches tall.

A member of the Red Baron Squadron. Public Domain Photo courtesy of GetArchive.com

The Red Baron Squadron

In 1979, some Red Baron Pizza marketing guy dreamed up the coolest pizza promoting scheme in pizza-promoting-scheme history—The Red Baron Squadron. On the surface, creating an aerial

Totally Pizza

stunt team to promote pizza is the sort of idea that takes place on Casual Friday over a doobie and three gallons of margaritas. The brass at Red Baron had both the ambition and insight to embrace the concept's coolness and support it. This civilian air team flew four vintage Stearman biplanes painted in red and white. Stearmans were trainer planes for the military in World War II. Unlike the American armed forces, the Red Baron Squadron hot rodded its aircraft with 450-horsepower Wasp-Junior engines. They also sported an inverted oil system to make flying upside-down possible.

The Red Baron Squadron traveled the States, flying formation acrobatics not only to promote the company but also to raise cash for children's charities. It was based out of the Southwest Minnesota Regional Airport. In 2007, the company retired the squadron. At the time, it was the oldest civilian air team in the United States.

The Spy Who Froze Me

A great story in "*Spooked: Espionage in Corporate America*," by Adam L. Penenberg and Marc Barry, details the lengths pizza corporations (and others) go to spy on each other. When Schwan's got wind of Kraft's impending DiGiorno launch in the 1990s, the rival food corporation brought in an outside intelligence "consultant" to get the low-down on this new crust that promised to revolutionize frozen pizza. Large companies like Coca-Cola, Dow Chemical, and General Electric tend to have CI (short for "competitive intelligence") units to handle all of their legal spying. Some of the people in corporate spying (not to be confused with its illegal cousin, corporate espionage) are even former CIA. Usually these spies-for-hire are brought in to find out such exciting info as marketing plans, factory production capacity, or R and D.

Schwan's didn't have an in-house CI department. They didn't even have an old British guy making cool cars with machine guns or exploding pens that

Espionage takes many forms and shows up where you least expect it...like in the pizza industry. Spy vs. Spy Cos Play at NYC Comic Con 2012. Photo by Marnie Joyce from New York City, USA, CC BY 2.0, via Wikimedia Commons

Totally Pizza

also unzip a femme fatale's dress. What they *did* have was a smart guy armed with a telephone, which is all he needed in order to give Schwan and its pizza company, Freschetta, a huge boost in catching up to DiGiorno. Freschetta already had its own version of self-rising frozen crust in the works. The problem wasn't in figuring out how to make the pizza work; they already knew that DiGiorno's secret was pumping yeast into the crust. What Schwan's needed was a timetable. If they were to have any chance of closing the gap with Kraft, they needed to know when DiGiorno was going into nationwide distribution.

The consultant had to learn all he could about the DiGiorno factory's production capacity, from its square footage to the types of equipment and the sizes and types of pizza being produced. Walking into the place and just asking around wasn't going to get the job done. You don't get to be the size of Kraft without knowing how to guard your secrets. What's more, the Society of Competitive Intelligence Professionals (aka SCIP), which governs CI industry operatives like some corporate Geneva Convention, forbids deception when talking to a target on the job. Thus, the outsourced needed an outsource—specifically, someone akin to what the Mafia calls a "zip"—an outsider who comes in for a job, then leaves, giving his employer plausible deniability. Bringing in a non-SCIP operative got around that whole silly "spy, but be honest" rule.

Using a pre-paid phone card from a convenience store, fake voice mail, and a fax line all set in New York, the spy didn't even have to leave town to do the job. Over the course of his operation, he posed as a reporter, an environmentalist, and the owner of a cardboard box plant, as he tracked down the information through the Sussex Chamber of Commerce, the building inspector's office, accounts payable at the factory itself, and eventually the plant manager.

Between his fancy phone work and masterful use of the Internet, the spy gathered so much vital information that not only was Schwan's able to formulate an aggressive plan, Freschetta rapidly rose the number two spot behind DiGiorno in one of the fastest-growing segments of the pizza industry at the time.

How many frozen pizzas are sold each year in the United States?
A. 500 million
B. 400 million
C. 700 million
D. 600 million
Correct Answer: C. 700 million

Totally Pizza

Half Stoned, Fully Baked

Chicago food writer Pat Bruno tells his version of the pizza stone's origin, and it's actually kind of cool. He claims that while hanging out with the legendary Julia Child during a pizza making session in the oven, she said the crust would be much crisper if someone could just get some ceramic tile from the stone yard and break it up so it fit into a roasting pan. Bruno says that inspired his idea for a single stone designed just for pizza baking in the oven.

The reason Juila lamented getting stoned was heat distribution. By using a flat stone or piece of ceramic under pizza or other baked bread goods, you get a really sweet even distribution of heat, just like in a masonry oven. Porous rock also absorbs moisture making for a crisper crust.

Small pizza stones can be purchased to fit in any conventional cooking oven or an enclosed barbecue-style grill . High-end ovens sometimes offer optional pizza stones that are specifically designed for each oven model and may include a specialized heating element. A home made "pizza stone" can also be made by distributing one or two layers of unglazed tiles on top of an oven rack.

Just don't place a cold stone in a hot oven. That's what causes thermal shock and fractures your rock. You want to put the stone into the oven while both are still cold and let them heat together for at least 45 minutes. Likewise, you should also let the hot stone cool in the oven after cooking to avoid the same problem.

Pizza by the Acre

Pizza doesn't grow on trees, but it does grow on farms. Here and in the U. K. you can find pizza farms—educational attractions that grow all the ingredients needed for pizza, including the meat. It's usually a small farm on a circular spread of land that's partitioned into slice-shaped plots for growing the various ingredients (wheat for crust, tomatoes for sauce, dairy cows for cheese, herbs, and pigs for pork pepperoni). Some have access to coal or natural gas deposits for heating fuel, too.

Part IV

Extra Cheese

Supreme pizza. Public domain image courtesy of US Department of Agriculture, modified by Scott Bauer, via Wikimedia Commons

The Pizza Connection:
Crime by the Slice

"The zips are Sicilians brought into this country to distribute heroin. They set up pizza parlors, where they received and distributed heroin, laundered money. The zips were clannish and secretive...the meanest killers in the business." —FBI agent Joe Pistone, quoting a conversation with a Bonanno crime family member while Pistone was undercover with the family

Just like when you lay with dogs you get fleas, when you hang around with criminals a lot, there's a good chance criminal shit is going to go down in your vicinity. That's why it's no shocker that plenty of other crimes have happened in or around mob-influenced businesses, including some pizzerias. It's not the pizza parlor's fault. You can't say, "Look at the checkered tablecloths and the guy with the Mario Bros mustache. That pizzeria was begging for it." Well, you can, but all that really tells people is what a small-minded, ignorant pizza bigot you are (or a smarmy, jackass author with a sick sense of humor). No, buildings are innocent pawns of whatever tenants take up residence/business under their warm, welcoming roofs. Some of those businesses are restaurants, and some of those restaurants fall under the iron grip of organized crime, usually via money laundering or extortion.

That's because restaurants are a cash-intensive industry. Cash comes in, cash goes out. Thus, they're an excellent middle stop between drug dealing (or prostitution or gambling) and the bank. For the few of us out there who've never fibbed on our taxes, here's how this sort of money laundering works: Crime boss A can't go to the bank and deposit his money directly into the bank, since the pesky scamps at the IRS will want to know how he earned his income and they won't just take his word for it when he states that it fell off of a truck. He gets around this unfortunate quirk of the government via High-Cash Business B, which deposits his money for him as business earnings. Hence, Crime Boss A's dirty money is clean as soon as it leaves the laundromat (which, in this case is someplace like a strip club, tanning salon, parking garage,

Totally Pizza

or a restaurant). High-cash businesses are operations where customers tend to pay with actual currency as opposed to credit/debit cards, or, for those of you just joining us in the Information Age, checks. Pizzerias definitely fall into this category.

Most restaurants are law-abiding establishments but their cash-on-hand nature makes them attractive for all kinds of other evil, and not the fun kind with latex and nipple wax. In fact, pizza delivery is one of the most dangerous jobs in America, not just because of other drivers texting and shaving, either. Drivers are often mugged for the wads of cash they collect while making deliveries. In some cases, desperate people want the food itself. In others, the delivery order is a cover for some extremely bad intentions toward the driver.

But wait—there's more. Pizza played mob accomplice for the largest mafia trial in history, Al Capone allegedly had his fingers in the mozzarella industry, and then there are all the scams (as well as acts of violence) committed by rival pizzerias against one another. Between 1975 and 1984 the Mafia distributed huge amounts of cocaine and heroin here in the U. S., then laundered the profits before sending the cash to the suppliers in Sicily. The front for this enterprise? A number of independent pizzerias in the Northeast and Midwestern United States.

These pizza parlors were the cover for drug sales and collections. At the huge mega-trial that ensued, evidence proved that over $1.6 billion in heroin exchanged hands this way during that nine-year period. Hence the term, "Pizza Connection," which would later be applied to the trial itself. Or, to put it in pop culture terms, American, Italian, and Swiss law enforcement did more damage to the real Mafia drug trade in one big operation than the writers of Miami Vice did to the fictional drug trade in five seasons of television. Suck on that, stylish `80s TV detectives.

A mammoth two-year investigation by American and Italian authorities culminated in dozens of coordinated arrests in Italy, Spain, Switzerland, and the United States on April 9, 1984. This well-orchestrated arrest-fest came on the heels of Gaetano Badalmenti's (and several family members) apprehension in Madrid the day prior. Badalmenti was the former boss of the Sicilian La Cosa Nostra, and a key supplier of heroin and cocaine to the U. S. Mafia distributors. No fewer than four branches of law enforcement conducted the American arrests alone: the FBI, DEA, U. S. Customs Service, and the NYPD. The level of cooperation between U.S law enforcement, the Italian National Police, Italian prosecutors, and Swiss authorities was extremely close and intense, even sharing highly sensitive information in a team effort to cripple the U. S./Italian Mafia narcotics business.

Of the 38 mafia members and associates that originally were indicted in the case, 27 of the defendants lived in the U. S. at the time of the arrests. Twenty-two

Totally Pizza

of them eventually stood trial in one courtroom, at the same time. And that was believed to be just the tip of the cocaine iceberg. No one really knows exactly how many Mafiosi were involved in the entire operation. Three of the accused were iced before the trial ended—one defendant was murdered before it even started, one died of natural causes, and the third got whacked during the trial.

Tommaso Buscetta taken into custody by the Italian police. Photo courtesy of cosanostranews.com.

Which, by the way, set a record as the longest federal jury trial in a criminal action. All of the defendants were Sicilian born, many couldn't speak English, and each had his own defense attorney. Presenting the prosecution's case took a year in and of itself. You'd think that chewing such a large legal morsel would have confused the jury, but this wasn't found to be the case, even on appeal. All but one of the defendants was convicted and only one verdict got overturned on appeal. Since the whole point of the case was to send a message to the drug trade, authorities let the scale and costs of the trial skyrocket. By the time the dust settled, the trial's bill weighed in at $50 million.

Gaetano Badalamenti was the Mafia whale caught in the prosecution's net. He was a Mafioso of the old school—*omerta*, the code of slience, was as sacred to him as a cow in India or beef in Texas. When Cosa Nostra restructured the Mafia Commission in Sicily in 1970 as a triumvirate, Badalmenti was one of the three dons charge.

Peace lasted less than five years, if it existed at all. The Corleonese faction drove Badalmenti into exile in 1981. Seeing as how the Corleonesi murdered eleven of Badalamenti's relatives (including two nephews in New Jersey and a third shot and hacked to bits), his fears were well founded. Badalmenti broke camp and fled Sicily as much for his family's protection as for his own. Some of Baldamenti's clan were distributing heroin via pizzerias they ran in the Midwest. The operation was huge. The Sicilians handled the heroin trade, giving kickbacks to the American mobsters for running the business for them. At least some of the heroin was smuggled in alongside cheese, tomatoes, and olive oil.

The drugs weren't the only Sicilian export entering America illegally. A workforce of Sicilian Mafiosi slipped into the States undetected. Many of those who came over illegally were Italian fugitives fleeing a range of charges in their motherland ranging from drug trafficking to murder. In the Sixties and Seventies these guys, known as "zips," built the heroin network. Law enforcement first thought they were part of the Bonanno family. The truth is that American mobsters were only too happy to let the Sicilians do all the heavy lifting as long as they got their cut. This Mafia money machine didn't last forever. In 1984, the U. S. and Italy teamed up to smash it here and abroad, resulting in the massive trial dubbed The Pizza Connection. New extradition and assistance treaties allowed law enforcement from both nations to team up and share information in fun, new ways.

After he failed to kill himself in an Italian prison in 1983, Sicilian Mafioso Tommaso Buscetta had had enough of Cosa Nostra. Between fleeing the law, doing time in prison, and even being tortured by the military regime in Brazil, he felt it was time for a life change. Part of this new life included breaking *omerta*—in a very big way. Not only did Buscetta start talking, he painted a full picture. Buscetta confirmed the existence of the Sicilian Mafia Commission—clear evidence of just how big and organized the Mafia was back then. American and Italian law enforcement now understood the true nature of the mob beast and created the extradition and assistance pact needed to attack it more effectively than ever before. His testimony during the Pizza Connection played a big part in convicting the defendants. Afterward he allegedly underwent plastic surgery before going into witness protection.

Information gold mine that Buscetta was, he still wasn't the star witness. That title goes to fellow Mafioso Salvatorre Contorno. At first he'd have no part of it, but after Buscetta convinced him to turn informant, Contorno gave testimony directly linking the defendants to dealing heroin. According to Contorno, he was there at meeting in Sicily in 1980 where five of the defendants "took out two plastic garbage bags and extracted packages of white powder in clear plastic envelopes, each bearing different tiny scissor cuts or pen or pencil marks to identify the individual owner. They poured samples of the powder into a bottle heating on a hot plate." The samples were later seized by the DEA.

The Pizza Connection was also quite a feather in the cap of the United States Attorney for the Southern District of New York, whose support and assistance proved vital to the case—just as it would decades later when he was Mayor of New York City during one of its darkest hours. Most of us know that lawyer, Rudy Giuliani, for his efforts in the wake of 9/11, but before that he was also very involved in the execution of the largest Mafia narcotics case in American history.

Obviously, The Pizza Connection didn't nuke the mafia all the way back to the Stone Age. We don't hear about large scale operations busting hundreds of mobsters anymore, but incidents in the pizza industry still occur from time to time. I'll give you two examples from 2009. Apparently, pizza extortion hasn't gone away. In July 2009, Lenny Palermo died in Washington Township, New Jersey. He'd owned Lenny's Brick Oven Pizzeria and Restaurant. Two days later, a guy named John Koster, who hung out at Lenny's, told the general manager that Koster was now going to run the place and that the boss was going to stop by for a little chat. "The boss" turned out to be Francesco "Frank" Guaracci, the reputed head of the DeCavalcante crime family. Right around 9 pm, the mob boss and his goons showed up, demanded the manager give Koster the day's cash and the restaurant's recipes, and bullied him when the manager refused. Eventually, one of the customers who fled the place called the police, resulting in arrests for the offenders. Lenny's closed about a year and a half after the incident.

My second tale is one of calzone and cocaine. In April 2009, the *New York Daily News* ran a story about a Bronx pizza parlor named John's Pizza, which allegedly employed its drivers as drug runners to ferry cocaine shipments throughout the city. Six people, including the manager, were arrested as a result.

"That's the Chicago Whey!"
All cheesy dialogue references to *The Untouchables* aside, even Al Capone had his mitts in pizza's pie. The late investigative journalist Jonathan Kwitny wrote about it in his book, *Vicious Circles: The Mafia in the Marketplace*. According to the story, Capone and fellow mobster Joe Bonanno controlled dairy farms and the Grande Cheese Company near Fond du Lac, Wisconsin.

Capone and Bonanno muscled in on Grande starting in 1941. The next six years were a bad time to be associated with the previous management or its competition. Unless, of course, you wanted a violent death. In that case, you were in luck. Over that period at least six such people met their bloody ends. Thomas O. Neglia, whose name was on Grande's incorporation papers, went into a barbershop for a shave in 1943 and got murdered while in the barber's chair. Rival cheesemaker Sam Gervasi was killed in a repair shop in 1944; later that same year James V. De Angelo, who'd expressed interest in Grande, wound up in his wife's trunk, his skull crushed. Not to be outdone, Anofrio Vitale, another name on Grande's incorporation paperwork, ended up in the Chicago sewers the next year. Vincent Benevento, aka the "cheese king,"

Totally Pizza

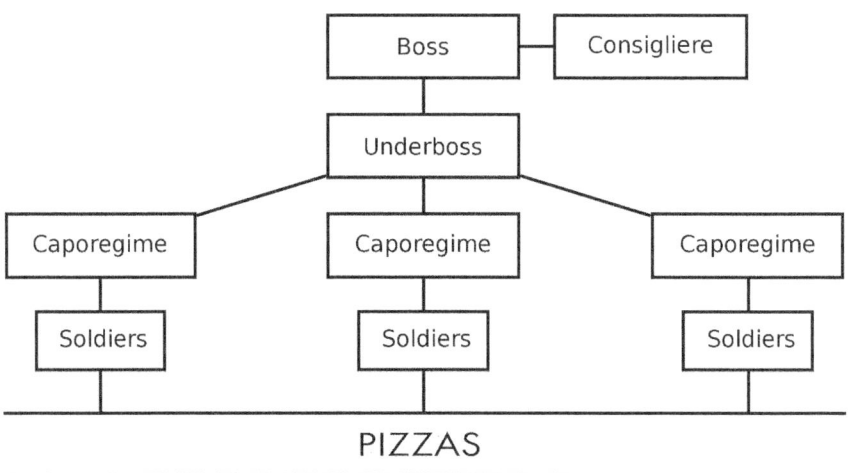

Mafia family structure tree (slightly modified). Public Domain image.

caught five rounds of lead in front of his business in Wisconsin. The last of the six was Nick DeJohn, who'd ventured into the mozzarella trade without the mob's blessing. He was found dead in the trunk of a car in San Francisco in 1947.

What's more, a 1980 study conducted by the Pennsylvania Crime Commission makes some very specific accusations about the mob and the pizza industry. It states: "The most incriminating tie to Organized Crime though is the fact that Roma Foods utilizes the services of Salvatore Profaci as an enforcer of territorial rights and full-time "consultant." The Crime Commssion investigation has established that Profaci, a member of the Colombo organization and son of the late crime boss Joseph Profaci of New York, has threatened other suppliers and has handled labor disputes for Roma Foods associated company in New Jersey. Profaci, whose first contact with Roma Foods came in 1971 as a representative of Grande Cheese, operates out of an office at the Roma Foods warehouse. Employees and suppliers to Roma have told Pennsylvania Crime Commission investigators that Profaci seems to control the company. Profaci also is a "sales agent" for Lisanti Foods which is associated with Roma Foods as the northern New Jersey pizza supply distributor." There's no evidence that either company is currently connected to the Mafia, however.

Grande is still making cheese to this very day. Management has stated as far back as the late `70s or early `80s that the last stock owned by the Mafia was bought out and that the mob's influence has long since been purged from its business dealings. Yeah, that's what I'd say if I were them.

114

Totally Pizza

Identity Theft, Straight to Your Door

Central Florida is a tourism gold mine. Between the resort hotels, Disney World, time shares, and vacation homes, it's the place to be if you're a gator with a taste for tourists—or an identity thief.

Some enterprising scumbag came up with the novel idea of using pizza delivery flyers without all the work of keeping up his end of the bargain (like actually making or delivering a pizza). You call the fake number on the flyer, give your credit number, and thirty minutes later, you're still hungry. Meanwhile, the crook on the other end of the line gets busy destroying your credit rating. Criminals employ young people to put the flyers on hotel, resort, and time share doors. Sometimes organized criminals even encourage them to test the room doors to see if they're locked, in hopes of burglarizing the place.

The situation got so bad that lawmakers passed the Pizza Flyer Act. Not only does it increase the criminal penalties for thieves running the operation it also uses civil forfeiture to confiscate the vans used to transport the young thieves to the hotels.

Nobody Likes a Rat

A pizza man in Upper Darby, Pennsylvania thought it would be whimsical to dabble in a little crime on the side. Unfortunately, he failed the first rule of crookery—look for cops first. The pizzeria owner went into a rival pizza joint, placed two mice in the dining room, then moseyed on over to another pizzeria to put more mice in its garbage cans. The mastermind might have had great success if he hadn't placed the first two mice *right in front* of two cops who were having lunch at the first pizzeria at the time. The police then arrested him, most likely once they stopped laughing. His rivals accused the man of "food terrorism," whatever the hell that means.

Piece Talks

The Bonanno and Colombo crime families once had a sit-down over pizza. Not over a pizza—over pizza. I imagine there've been plenty of Mafia peace talks where a pizza was actually on the table. Only one I know of has been about a stolen pizza recipe.

In 2012, while testifying in a murder trial, a former Colombo *capo* said that his alleged associate got really pissed off when he thought his in-laws at L&B Spumoni Gardens had their pizza recipe hijacked by a new Staten Island pizzeria named The Square (the new pizza place was opened by the two sons of a Bonanno associate; they had worked at L&B). In fact, the two mafia families had to have a sit-down to avoid a gangland war. At first, the Colombo Mafiosi wanted $75,000 but eventually the price dropped to $4,000. The Bonanno clan probably figured it was a deal, considering they would be able to avoid all those costly trunk-cleaning bills.

Dude, Don't Bogart the Cheese

In a gallant attempt to disprove stereotypes about Italians and organized crime, two black men from Ohio smuggled $421,000 worth of weed inside bundles of pizza cheese. They were busted at a Super 8 Motel near Phoenix while moving bundles of marijuana wrapped in the cheese from a semi and a van in the motel lot. For those of you keeping score at home, that's 823 pounds of herb.

Burn Notice

In fairness, not all pizza-related crime involves the Mafia. Some of it is just good old-fashioned, isolated-incident stuff. Like the two Domino's managers in Florida who thought they could beat the competition...by setting it on fire. Allegedly, the two Domino's employees thought they'd increase sales by burning down a competing Papa John's. Anything to avoid working harder to make sales, right guys?

Canadian Bakin'

"If you want to commit suicide in Montreal, you make ricotta and mozzarella cheese. Nobody sells mozzarella cheese in this city unless it's Saputo. The whole operation is Mafia." That's the answer the New York State Liquor Authority got from the Montreal police when asking about the Saputo cheese operation back in 1971. Not only

Friolano cheese made by Saputo. Photo by VerifiedCactus, CC BY-SA 4.0 via Wikimedia Commons

did Joe Bonanno have cheesy fingers in the States, he dipped into the mozzarella business up north, too.

In 1954 Bonanno bought 20% of Giuseppe Saputo & Sons, Ltd., Montreal stock for $8000. Nine years later, Santo Calderone thought it'd be a good idea to compete with Saputo by opening his own Montreal mozzarella operation. For his trouble, his trucks and equipment were vandalized, burned, or bombed, as

Totally Pizza

detailed in police reports about the incidents. Once acid was dropped into his fermenting milk, Calderone had had enough and closed up shop.

In the 1970's, Montreal Mafia goons acting as "sales reps" would go to small local pizza joints and insist that the owners buy their pizza ingredients from them in preset quotas (as a way of laundering money). It was a bad arrangement for the pizzeria owners, but for once a Mafia deal actually benefited the consumer. The shops didn't want all the extra ingredients to go to waste. As a result, Montreal pizza in the 1970s tended to have extra pepperoni and cheese on it—whether you ordered it that way or not.

Mob control over Montreal pizza faded away a long time ago. Recently, however, a cheese trafficking ring got busted in the Niagara area, run by some unusual perpetrators—cops.

Allegedly, a few enterprising police officers smuggled cases of brick cheese in their vehicle trunks from the United States and into Canada. With U.S cheese costing a third of what it does in Canada, the smugglers would sell it to pizzerias on the cheap, reportedly making $1000-$2000 a run. Brick cheese is often used as a pizza topping. Authorities came across the cheese smuggling via information gathered by the U.S. Department of Homeland Security during an arrest for conspiracy to smuggle anabolic steroids into Canada.

The Fast and the Furiously Hungry

Nine teens got busted for stealing at least 26 Honda Accords in Oakland and from BART stations in California's Contra Costa County over a two-month period. All police had to do was follow the pizza. Apparently, they were too stupid or lazy to learn from every CSI episode ever made—always clean up the crime scene when you leave. Investigators spotted a pattern to the thefts. The culprits drove the cars around for a few days while munching on pizza, then abandoned the Hondas—with the boxes and crusts still inside. Since the boxes all had the pizzeria's name on them but no purchase receipts, alert police reasoned that at least one of the thieves worked at the parlor in question.

Tracing the boxes back to an Oakland pizza joint, the cops busted the first of the nine suspects when they found him working the counter there. One other piece of evidence proved key as well—a scrap of paper with a name on it, inside a schoolbook in one of the stolen cars. Law enforcement tracked that back to a local high school where they spotted yet another stolen Accord in the lot. When one of the students got into the car, detectives nabbed him.

He'd actually bought The Club steering lock to protect his prize from theft.

117

Totally Pizza

Would the Real San Marzano Tomatoes Please Stand Up?
Because San Marzano's tomatoes are premium product, they have pricing to match. Place a counterfeit label on a can of generic tomatoes, and you can make a fortune. In 2010 alone, Italian authorities seized 1470 tons of canned tomatoes carrying counterfeit labels impersonating San Marzano brands. The tomatoes had a street value of 1.2 million euros.

Pie Spy
There's an urban legend about a group of FBI agents who tried to order a bunch of pizzas while investigating at a psychiatric hospital, only to be hung up on in disbelief by the pizzeria on the other end of the call. According to Snopes.com, it's absolutely true. While the Southwood Psychiatric Hospital in San Diego was being investigated for medical insurance fraud, the bureau conducted a search and seizure of its rooms and financial records. The approximately sixty agents involved got a tad hungry, so the agent in charge called a local pizzeria to order up some delivery grub. According to one agent, the phone conversation went a lot like this:

Agent: "Hello. I'd like to order nineteen large pizzas and sixty-seven cans of soda."

Pizzeria: "Okay, where would you like us to deliver them?"

Agent: "The Southwood Psychiatric Hospital."

Pizzeria: "Uh... huh... To the psychiatric hospital, you say?"

Agent: "That's right. I'm an FBI agent."

Pizzeria: "You're an FBI agent?"

Agent: "Correct. Just about everybody here is."

Pizzeria: "Sure, sure. And you're at the psychiatric hospital?"

Agent: "Yes. Oh, and don't go through the front doors. We have them locked. You'll have to go around to the back to the service entrance."

Pizzeria: "Riiight. And you say you're all FBI agents?"

Agent: "That's right. How soon can you have them here? We've been here all day and we're starving."

Pizzeria: "Okay. How are you going to pay for this?"

Agent: "I have my check book right here."

Pizzeria: "You say all of you are FBI agents? At the psychiatric hospital?"

Agent: That's right, everyone here is. Can you remember to bring the pizzas and sodas to the service entrance in the rear? We have the front doors locked."

Pizzeria: "I'll pass."

Click.

Ultimately, the feds got their pizza. They just had to send a few agents to pick it up.

Totally Pizza

14

The Rise of Gourmet and Artisan Pizza

"It's not your pizza, it's mine. You don't pay until the end of the meal. Until then, it's mine." —Artisan pizzaiolo Chris Bianco

By the 1980s, pizza had gone worldwide—thanks largely to corporations like Pizza Hut and Domino's. It's true that Italian immigrants to other parts of the world had taken pizza with them when they left their homeland during the late nineteenth and early twentieth centuries, but it was the standardized, American corporate machine that popularized pizza around the globe. That was the good news.

The bad news was that in the process, pizza was typecast as a B-list performer: a generic bread topped with equally generic cheese, sauce, meat and veggies. If you had one pepperoni pizza from a chain, you'd pretty much had 'em all. True believers in Italy and serious pizza *aficionados* alike chafed under that misconception. That's what gave rise to the AVPN in Naples and ultimately led to American *pizzaiolos* questing for pizza's real roots here in the States, giving rise to artisan pizza. Other chefs saw the creative potential in pizza and took it out of the homogenous fast food realm and into the world of fine dining. That's where California-style/gourmet pizza enters the picture.

Ed LaDou, aka The Prince of Pizza, had a long history with pizza years before he started experimenting with it. In the 1970s, LaDou learned the pizza-maker's craft as a teenager at Frankie, Johnnie & Luigi Too, a traditional New York-style pizzeria in Mountain View, California. Later on His Highness made pizzas at Ecco, an upscale restaurant in Palo Alto, California. By the time Ed started at Prego, a restaurant specializing in old-school thin-crust Italian pizza, he knew his way around a pizza oven pretty damn well. The chefs let the young *pizzaiolo* play with toppings like prosciutto, goat cheese, and truffles in their wood-burning oven. They'd even send the results to guests for feedback.

One of those adventurous guests was Wolfgang Puck.

Ed's off-menu experiment, topped with ricotta, mustard, paté, and red pepper,

119

Totally Pizza

made its way to a table occupied by Puck and his girlfriend at the time, designer Barbara Lazaroff. Recognizing LaDou's special gift, the famous chef put him in charge of pizza at a little place in Los Angeles named Spago. Under Puck's guidance, LaDou developed more than 250 pizza concepts using a Christmas list of ingredients no Neapolitan *pizzaiolo* or corporate test kitchen would ever contemplate putting on a pizza. Things like scallops, fish roe, and baby zucchini flowers all made their way into Ed LaDou's arsenal of pizza toppings. Other innovations included using infused olive oil, baby vegetables, chile oil, and flavored dough. Based on the success of his pizzas and his status as a celebrity chef, Puck opened a series of restaurants, ranging from high-end clones of Spago to convenience chains for airports and mall food courts.

While Ed LaDou was going Hollywood, Alice Waters was busily refining the

California-style pizza from the Chez Panisse cafe in Berkeley, California.
Photo courtesy of Pizetta, via Wikimedia Commons

California cuisine she'd created at Chez Panisse alongside head chef Jeremiah Tower. It was a style that mixed Italian and French techniques with fresh, local ingredients. When she came back from a trip to Italy, Alice created an open kitchen with a wood-burning pizza oven as its focal point. Chez Panisse baked the pizzas and calzones in the classical Italian fashion but, true to form, topped their single-serving dishes with things like duck and goat cheese. Success came instantly and with it, many happy food critics.

Between corporate pizza's standardized pies and gourmet pizza's totally innovative approach to pizza, people lost track of its roots. That's one of the reasons Neapolitans started that bastion of pizza purity, the AVPN. Pizza purists quested

Totally Pizza

back through pizza's history to recover the lost essence of traditional pizza, and Chris Bianco became the face of that movement, which we now know as artisan pizza.

The Baird Machine Shop built in 1920. It now houses Pizzeria Bianco. It was listed in the National Register of Historic Places in 1985 Phoro by Marine 69-71 at English Wikipedia, CC BY-SA 3.0, via Wikimedia Commons

Pizzeria Bianco is his baby, and the story of its origin story would do a Naples pizza shop proud. Why? Modesty, my friend. When Pizzeria Bianco fired up its oven in 1987, it was in a grocery store, which later became AJ's Euro-Market & Deli in Phoenix, Arizona. Nowadays you'll find it in Heritage Square, which has been Pizzeria Bianco's home digs since 1996. Chris Bianco was born in the Bronx and had asthma as a child. The condition kept him cooped up inside, but that gave him plenty of time to learn from his aunt's cooking. Like Ed LaDou, he learned how to make pizza as a teenager at the local pizza parlor. But where LaDou moved into experimenting with all kinds of funky stuff on his pizzas, Bianco went the other direction. In fact, his story is so tied to old-school pizza it is easy to understand why he brought Old World craftsmanship out West with him when he moved to Phoenix in 1985. Anyone who makes mozzarella from his apartment for sale to Italian restaurants like Chris did is pretty well on the path to becoming a classic *pizzaiolo*.

Guy Coscos, a specialty grocer in Phoenix, liked Chris Bianco's cheese so much he offered him the chance to sell his own pizzas in the corner of Cosco's store. Bianco hasn't looked back since. Although he did look forward, especially to the pilgrimage he made to Italy in 1993 to hone his craftsmanship. It was a lot like an American kung fu student going to China to learn at the feet of the Shaolin masters, only with more dough and fewer bad guys getting their asses kicked.

Totally Pizza

Today Pizzeria Bianco is nationally recognized for its pizzas. The joint's small seating capacity means long wait times, the place sports a wood-burning oven, and Bianco himself still makes the homemade mozzarella cheese used on the pizzas. He says, "There's no mystery to my pizza. Sicilian oregano, organic flour, San Marzano tomatoes, purified water, mozzarella I learned to make at Mike's Deli in the Bronx, sea salt, fresh yeast cake, and a little bit of yesterday's dough. In the end great pizza, like anything else, is all about balance. It's that simple."

Sink Your Moose's Tooth Into This Pizza

A million years ago when I was in college, a fellow student with more money than brains asked me, "You're from Alaska? Did you, like, live in an igloo?"

"Yep," I replied, "and it had a two car garage and cable TV, just like all the igloos down here."

Her ignorance wasn't surprising. Not many people knew much about my home state aside from the stereotypes. Thanks to an ex-governor with more money than brains, they still don't; most folks just have a different set of stereotypes to go on now, thanks to her time in the national spotlight. In reality, there's much more to Alaskans than idiots claiming to see Russia from their houses. Anchorage is home to the highest-grossing indie pizzeria in the world—The Moose's Tooth. When I found that out, I was blown away (and very proud of my hometown).

Tipping the scale at over $6 million gross a year, The Moose's Tooth may be the heaviest pizza hitter you've never heard of. Rod Hancock and Matt Jones passed up promising careers in the corporate world for the noblest of reasons, pizza and

Moose's Tooth logo, Ancorage, Alaska.

beer. They were rock climbers without an ounce of restaurant experience between them when they launched Moose's Tooth Pub and Pizzeria back in 1996. Jones and Hancock had no clue just how deep the rabbit hole would go, and they got knocked around a bit learning the ropes. Rod was considering a sweet job offer from Microsoft while Matt, an Anchorage boy like yours truly, had just passed the Alaska bar exam when the duo decided they didn't want to work for The Man. Between Hancock's love of

Totally Pizza

cooking and Jones' ventures into bathtub brewing, what they lacked in restaurant know-how they made up for with garage band-esque enthusiasm and desire. Both also loved the gourmet pizzas and microbrews from their Portland college days.

After a lot of planning and pleas from stressed out parents to abort, the Moose's Tooth opened up shop at a spot in Anchorage that's killed many a dream—the place where the Old Seward Highway ends near the New Seward. Lots of restaurants have died there over the years, slain by poor location. This didn't bode well. Moose's Tooth 1.0 was a pretty modest operation. It had one employee: a cook to crank out Rod's pizzas. There wasn't even an ordering system. Tickets landed in front of the cook in no particular order, and pizzas went out the same way. As for the brewery part, it consisted of old dairy vats in an old steam plant offsite. Still, The Moose's Tooth sold 80 pies on opening night. Marketing consisted of a "Grand Opening" banner and word-of-mouth via friends and family (some of whom waited tables during the first couple weeks). The number of pizzas grew to over 500 a day, *without* a delivery service. Matt and Rod had borrowed $130,000 interest-free from parents and friends. By the end of that first year, it was repaid in full. Only a few beer choices were available, but that grew to 20 custom beers created by Jones.

The owners also instituted something called "First Tap." Whenever they introduced a new beer, a local band was brought in to entertain during the launch party. Anchorage not being the largest city on Earth, Hancock and Jones ran out of local talent and started booking national acts at their other venue—Bear Tooth, and in other locales in town. At one point, the band Korn came to them to book two shows that ended up selling 8,000 tickets. Like California Pizza Kitchen, The Moose's Tooth has really grown up and expanded, most likely beyond the first vision of its creators. It just doesn't have that slimy corporate film stuck to it.

Dude, Watch This...

Those words, which have prefaced every bad idea that's ever sent a teenage boy to the emergency room, have also kicked off some pretty cool ideas. I don't think Ed LaDou or Alice Waters actually said them when they created gourmet pizza independently of each other in 1980, but the sentiment was probably there.

Overall, the idea mates New York-style crust with California-style toppings. Now, you'll find it in all kinds of places because as often happens with a cool idea, it makes a big pile of money, goes corporate, and becomes the standard that it was originally created to rebel against. In this case, California Pizza Kitchen, Extreme Pizza, and Sammy's Woodfired Pizza are three of the major pizza franchises associated with California-style pizza.

Totally Pizza

Two Lawyers, A Chef, and a Pizza Place

Richard L. Rosenfeld and Larry S. Flax knew very little about the restaurant business when they started their new eatery idea in 1985, California Pizza Kitchen. That's probably why they recruited the Prince of Pizza to help. Not only did Ed LaDou bring years of experience to the table, he also brought a lot of the recipes he'd created at Spago. Like his old gig, CPK utilized open kitchens centered on wood-burning pizza ovens. The difference was in the ingredients. Where Spago went all exotic and chi-chi, CPK focused on comfort food for toppings. The real fun didn't start until a month before opening. That's when CPK's new chef thought it'd be a good idea to quit. Ed stepped in and designed the entire menu. In the process, he invented the barbecue pizza that helped make the place famous.

Between CPK and Wolfgang Puck, California pizza is now a national cuisine. They transformed it from trendy curiosity to mass-marketed food. Both make frozen pizzas, although CPK has had more success in that area because it's backed by the juggernaut that is Kraft.

A Slice of Kosher

One of Ed LaDou's most famous creations was Jewish Pizza—a cooked pie topped with smoked salmon, crème fraîche, capers, and dill.

Quiz

Up until 2010, Chris Bianco still baked the majority of pizzas himself. How many did he make in a night?
A. Up to 250
B. Up to 150
C. A little over 200
D. Just under 300
Correct Answer: A. Up to 250

How long does Pizzeria Bianco let its handmade pizza dough ferment?
A. 12 hours
B. 10 hours
C. 22 hours
D. 16 hours
E. 18 hours
Correct Answer: E. 18 hours

Pizza, International Food of Mystery

"I would think if the Chicago Mafia came to Australia today, they would probably think that it was full of blokes who go around wrestling crocodiles—whether that be Crocodile Dundee or Steve Irwin. But one thing they would not be wondering about is where they could go to get a pizza." —Bryan Brown, actor

A little over a thousand years ago, the Vikings raided all over Europe. Right around 1970, the Romans returned the favor when pizza invaded Sweden. It hitched a ride with the influx of Italian guest workers who came to work in Sweden at that time, became popular, and thrived. Scandinavia didn't leave this Italian import stock, either. They customized it every bit as much as Americans did in the United States.

Taking the hot rod analogy a step further, Swedish *pizzaiolos* left the chassis stock but tweaked everything else; Neapolitan crust made a great foundation for all kinds of new and interesting toppings. Margherita and other Naples styles all have places of honor in Viking country but with variations better suited to the cultural tastes of the region. Pizza Margherita uses dried oregano and a Swedish hard cheese instead of the customary fresh basil and buffalo mozzarella used in Naples. The differences don't end with a few cheese and herb swaps, either. A typical Swedish pizza menu has more characters than the Star Wars universe. Forty or fifty different pizza types are usually listed at Sweden's pizzerias, with some restaurant offerings even going as high as one hundred recipes. Moreover, many Swedes eat their pies with a fork and knife.

Other European countries have their own tweaks, versions, and contributions to what has become, arguably, the world's favorite food. What's more, the further you get from Italy, the weirder pizza gets. At least to an ignorant Westerner like myself. Beyond Europe, pizza is, much like heavy metal music in the 1980s, big in Japan. It's popular all over Asia, but if you had to pick a central hub of popularity in the East, it's hard to beat the Japanese.

Totally Pizza

American pizza chains landed in Japan during the 1970s, when Shakey's and Pizza Hut opened up shop there in 1973. The Japanese not only embraced pizza, they ran with it—just like they've done with Western ideas since Perry's sea visit in 1859. Squid ink, mayonnaise, and seaweed all figure very prominently in Japan's pizza culture. Domino's followed its competition to Nippon in 1985. None of them, however, are the biggest kid on the block. That honor goes to a chain named Pizza-La. Headquartered in Japan, the company has stores in 37 of Japan's 43 prefectures.

Pizza-La food truck. Emran Kassim, CC BY 2.0, via Wikimedia Commons

Quiz

Pizza of Death is a record label in Japan. Which of these is not a band under said label?

A. Satanic Surfers

B. BBQ Chickens

C. Me First and the Gimme Gimmes

D. A Pizza the Action

Correct Answer: D. A Pizza the Action. Although it should be.

126

Totally Pizza

Swedish Meatballs (Hold the Meatballs)

This is actually one of the more interesting Swedish pies. Combining chicken, peanuts, pineapples, bananas, and far too much curry powder, it's a dollop of peanut butter away from being Pizza Elvis instead. For you kids under ninety out there, Elvis Presley was this guy who liked peanut butter-and-banana sandwiches. He was also kind of key to introducing White America to a thing called rock n' roll back in the 1950s. The Swedish version of Hawaiian pizza starts off normal enough—pineapple, ham. Then some bananas and curry. Still, no peanut butter. Why do you hate peanut butter, Sweden?

True or False: Kebab-pizza has been s so popular in Sweden since the 1990s that *Kebabpizza Slivovitza* was a song that actually made it into the Swedish Eurovision song contest back in 2008.
Correct Answer: True.

Quiz

Which of the following is *not* found in a traditional Swedish side salad for pizza?
A. Shredded cabbage
B. Carrots
C. Coarse pepper
D. Vinaigrette for pickling
Correct Answer: B. Carrots, much to the chagrin of pizza-loving Swedish rabbits.

Needs More Mint

Preferably, a breath mint. I'm not sure how Russia's *Mockba*—pizza topped with sardines, tuna, mackerel, onions, herring, and salmon—tastes, but I'm guessing fishy with some serious dragon breath afterward. It's traditionally served cold. When Pizza Hut opened its first pizzeria in Moscow back in 1990, *Mockba* (or, *Moskva*, depending on who you ask) was a huge local favorite. So much so that at one point the Moscow location was Pizza Hut's highest-volume unit in the world. Pizza Hut units in France, Hong Kong, Finland, and Britain weren't very far behind. However, Pizza Hut hasn't exactly enjoyed monumental success in Italy. Yeah, I know. I was shocked too.

Domino Theory

Not to be outdone, here are some of the pies Domino's Pizza offers in Europe to cater to local tastes:
Grilled Lamb (Netherlands)

Totally Pizza

Crème Fraiche (France)
Tuna and Sweet Corn (England)
Linguica and *Chorizo* (Portugal)

Tarte Flambee, France's idea of pizza pie. I prefer to call it Freedom Pie. Photo by Lulu Durand, CC BY 2.0, via Wikimedia Commons

French Tartes

France's Bas-Rhin region is home to *Tarte Flambee*, a popular pizza from that area in Alsace. It's made from a crepe-like dough topped with onion, bacon, and *crème fraiche*. Fried egg is also pretty popular on pizza throughout the country. It's either baked on top of the pizza or pan fried first, then put on top. Either way, sunny-side up is usually the name of that game.

European Sausagefest

You'd think Germans would be big into sausage on their pizza, given how many varieties of that meat are made there. While you'd be right (bratwurst being big on German pizza), canned tuna is also a local favorite on pizza there.

True or False

A 2004 AC Nielsen survey revealed Swedes eat more pizza per capita than anyone else in the world.

Totally Pizza

Correct Answer: False. The title actually went next door to Norway. The Norwegians ate 22,000 tons of frozen pizza alone that year. Home-baked pizza accounted for 15,000 tons, while 13,000 more tons came from restaurants.

"They Can Take Our Lives, but They Can Never Take Our Pizza!"

Not to be outdone by the lavish caviar-laden pie at Bellisima in New York, Restaurateur Domenico Crolla created one of the most expensive pizzas ever. It was topped by things like sunblush-tomato sauce, Scottish smoked salmon, medallions of venison, edible gold, lobster marinated in the finest cognac, champagne-soaked caviar, and the skins of milk-fed virgin puppies bred by the same Tibetans who trained Batman. That last ingredient is hotly disputed by the pizza community to this day. Next time I see Batman, I'll ask. What is known is that the pizza was auctioned for charity, raising £2,150 at the time.

Pizzaphrenic

Here's a quick list of pizza's multiple personalities that are popular in Europe:

Socca (aka "Farinata" or "cecina"): Often sold by the slice, this variety sports chickpea flour, water, salt and olive oil. In France's Provence region, it's known as *Socca*.

Pastrmajlija: Seeing as how this Macedonian bread pie is stuffed with meat and topped with even more meat, you vegetarian types probably aren't going to enjoy it. We predatory carnivores, on the other hand, like it quite well. Thank you, Macedonians.

Pissaladière: This Provençal pizza has a lot in common with its Italian cousins, only with a thicker crust. It's typically topped with onions, anchovies, and olives, making it a serious competitor with *Mockba* when it comes to causing halitosis.

Celtic Pie

While the traditional Irish favorites might make an interesting pizza, no one's in a rush to put potatoes, corned beef, and whiskey onto flatbread. At least, not in Ireland, where green peppers, onions, pepperoni, ham, sausage, spicy beef, mushrooms, sweet corn, and pineapple are the more popular toppings.

London Calling

A favorite topping combo in England is barbecue sauce, chicken, smoky bacon, onions and green peppers, served with a coleslaw appetizer. Works for me.

Totally Pizza

Telepizza
No, this is not what a set of annoying children's characters from the 1990s ate for dinner every night. Telepizza is a Spanish pizza chain sired by Leopoldo Fernández Pujals. In 1986 he inaugurated the first Telepizza in the Barrio del Pilar neighborhood in Madrid. It may not be nearly as huge as Domino's or Pizza Hut, but Telepizza has 1025 outlets worldwide, including 603 stores in Spain. It also has stores present in countries such as Portugal, Peru, Chile, Poland, Central America and United Arab Emirates. In June 2010 the company announced the arrival of the pizza chain to Colombia, where they bought Jeno's Pizza, achieving more than 80 restaurants throughout the country. Franchise pizza isn't just an American phenomenon, and Telepizza clearly illustrates that.

Twin Greeks
Traditionally, Greek pizza falls into one of two styles. The stereotypical version is topped with Kalamata olives, feta cheese, onion, tomato, gyro meat, spinach, and green bell pepper. As for the other, it refers to a type of oily crust that's baked in a pan, instead of Italian-style on the bricks in the oven proper. This type gets its label from the fact that it's usually found in pizza-and-pasta joints oftentimes run by Greek immigrants.

A Passage to India
Up until 1996, pizza in India meant dough dolloped with ketchup. That's when Domino's and Pizza Hut discovered what the British had known for centuries—that India was good for business. Both chains competed for this new market as heavily as two insecure teenage boys vying for the hottest girl in school. They really had to up their game to win consumer affections. At first they had different strategies. Where Domino's used its extensive experience to bring modern pizza delivery to the masses, Pizza Hut's draw was the dine-in pizzeria experience. They targeted the family demographic, especially kids. Both big chains prospered in India, but by 2000, Domino's alone had locations in every major city and town in the country.

Quiz
When the big chains hit India, they had to adjust their menus to fit local tastes. Which of the following pizzas was offered by Domino's?
A. Deluxe Chicken with Mustard Sauce and Sardines
B. Mutton *Ghongura* and Chicken *Chettinad*
C. Chicken *Pudina*

Totally Pizza

D. Butter chicken

E. All of the above

F. A and C.

Correct Answer: E. All of the above. Domino's offered nine India-specific pizzas in its first few years.

True or False: Domino's was the first to offer pizza delivery in India.

Correct Answer: False. A Delhi-based fast food chain, Nirula's, was the first to start free home delivery in 1994.

Kosher Any Way You Slice It (Or Not)

Unlike other countries where pizza companies have to deal with different culinary preferences, selling pizza in Israel adds the extra dimension of kosher versus non-kosher on a large scale. The big chains have both types of stores; kosher ones have no meat or use imitation meat to get around the Jewish prohibition of mixing meat and dairy. They also close during Passover, because no one's figured out how to make a good *matzah* pizza dough (*matzah* being the only bread product allowed at kosher restaurants during that holiday). Corn, *labane*, and Middle Eastern spices are among the toppings that set Israeli pizza apart from American or Italian. Israeli pizza is also known for much larger veggie portions than Americans might be used to.

Pizza with corn and za'atar at Pizza B'Riboa in Kfar Saba, Israel. Photo by Marc Resnick via Wikimedia Commons

The Boys from Brazil

Pizza is almost as old in São Paulo as it is in the United States—and is just as popular. The city sports 6,000 pizza establishments, and its residents eat a reported 1.4 million pizzas a day. The story goes that pizza first landed in Brazil during the early 20th

Totally Pizza

century in the Bras district of Sao Paulo. Pizza spread from Brazil's Italian communities at almost the same time it was leaving Little Italy's in the United States. Since then, pizza has exploded in popularity, with Neapolitan and Roman crust styles dominating. Traditional versions use tomato sauce and mozzarella as a base, although Brazilian pizza usually has less tomato sauce than its Italian counterpart. Brazilian pizzerias offer also Brazilian variants such as pizza topped with *catupiry* cheese. Sao Paulo loves pizza so much that July 10 is Pizza Day—it's the final day of an annual *pizzaiolo* competition.

True or False: *Catupiry* cheese was created by Portuguese monks to entice local natives to convert to Catholicism in the early 1600s.

Correct Answer: False. An Italian immigrant to Brazil named Mario Silvestrini came up with it in 1911. That lie about the monks sounds totally plausible, though, doesn't it?

Pizza, Gang Nam Style

Asia's other pizza capitol is South Korea, although the Philippines may dispute that with me. Either way, pizza is extremely popular in Korea, especially with young people. As in Japan, local pizza chains give America's Big Three serious competition for dominance (most notably, Mr. Pizza and Pizza Etang). You can get traditional pizza in Korea, and you can also get some takes on pizza that are so out of the ballpark as to be barely recognizable as pizza. Local foods like *bulgogi* (Korean barbecue) find their way onto pizza, as do others like potatoes, shrimp, crab, and corn.

Korea is the perfect example of how lovably crazy pizza can be. Just consider the super-deluxe "Grand Prix" at Mr. Pizza. Not only does it have Cajun shrimp, bell peppers, olives, and mushrooms on one side, it has potato wedges, bacon, crushed tortilla chips, and sour cream on the opposite. Oh, and its cookie dough crust is filled with potato mousse, then sprinkled with sunflower seeds, pumpkin seeds, and raisins. It also comes with blueberry dipping sauce. Not to be left behind, North Korea's first pizzeria opened up shop in Pyongyang in 2009.

16 Pizza in Pop Culture

Movies. Books. Video games. Toys. Pizza's resume includes appearances in all of these aspects of pop culture and more, besides. Centuries after the last pizza has rotted away in the remains of our society, future archaeologists will still know all about it by the sheer volume of plastic toys, games, DVDs, music files, and other pizza-related goods that illustrate just how far pizza has pervaded American society since Lombardi's first opened its doors in New York a little over a century ago. It's the clearest non-edible proof of our love for this most favorite of foods. Here are examples of popular culture that feature pizza, along with some choice quotes I've collected that sing the praises of pizza, the true American Pie.

Pizza: "I am the greatest!"

One magazine in 1977 reported that world champion boxer Muhammad Ali loved himself some pizza so much he considered installing a $55,000 pizza kitchen in his upscale $700,000 house. That's not surprising when you consider he loved chicken enough to open Ali's Trolley fast food cafe in the poor part of Chicago.

Liquid Pizza

In 1972, the actress Ann-Margaret fell from a giant mechanical hand during a stage show at the Sahara in Lake Tahoe. She suffered a concussion, broken arm, and had to have her jaw wired shut for months. It was perfect time to crave nice, chewy pizza. Fortunately, her husband, Roger Smith, had a kitchen appliance that liquified food. Into the blender went pizza. Oh, and roast lamb, hot dogs, and Swedish cakes.

Pizza Goes Hollywood

Seven decades after Lombardi's opened its doors in New York, Hollywood finally caught up and noticed pizza's star quality. Pizza's mostly been a bit player although it has starred in a couple of indie flicks in the last several years. But what it really wants to do is direct.

133

Totally Pizza

Saturday Night Fever (1977): This is the film that gave both John Travolta and pizza their big breaks. While Travolta peacocks through Brooklyn's mean streets, he's accessorized by pizza folded in the New York tradition.

Fast Times at Ridgemont High (1982): This teen comedy kick-started Sean Penn's career and in one of its most iconic scenes, he infuriates his teacher Mister Hand when the pizza he ordered is delivered during class. If ever pizza deserved a Best Supporting Actor nod, it was here—and the Academy snubbed it.

E.T. (1982): *Fast Times* did land pizza a walk-on gig in a Spielberg film so it wasn't all bad. What's more, pizza got a chance to do its own stunts when Henry Thomas steps on its box while discovering a Reese's Pieces-munching alien in the tool shed.

Mystic Pizza (1989): Seven years later, pizza starred opposite up-and-comer Julia Roberts centered around a Northeastern pizzeria renowned for its special sauce.

Do the Right Thing (1989): Spike Lee's racially-charged film partnered pizza with Lee as the protagonist tasked with delivering it. You could say *Do the Right Thing* did for pizza's acting career what *Pulp Fiction* did for Travolta's, but I wouldn't say it in front of Spike. He and Tarantino don't exactly get along.

A Japanese movie poster for Mystic Pizza. Image courtesy of Posterun.com

Goodfellas (1990): Pizza's oven finally got its first gig in this De Niro classic when mob thugs threaten to shove a mailman's head into the oven unless he stops delivering truancy letters to Ray Liotta's house.

Spider-Man 2 (2004): Pizza played a supporting cameo role when Tobey Maguire races to deliver it in 29 minutes or less.

Pizza (2005): Kylie Sparks and Ethan Embry co-starred with pizza in this independent film, which marks a return to pizza's modest roots before all that success went to its head. Or dough, or whatever.

Totally Pizza

Pizza (2012): Even Bollywood wants a slice of pizza, as evidenced by this Tamil thriller starring Vijay Sethupathi and Remya Nambesan.

Prime Time Pizza Down Under

Like many other great actors before, pizza has also taken its talents to the small screen. In Australia, it even had its own series on the SBS network. The show got a spin-off feature length film, *Fat Pizza*, released in 2003, and a best-of highlights video/DVD that featured previously unreleased footage and a schoolies exposé, released in 2004. In addition to this, a theater show entitled "Fat Pizza", starring several characters from the show, has toured the Australian east coast. Paul Fenech, who portrays the protagonist of the series—pizza deliveryman Pauly—also wrote and directed it.

...and Then There are the Teenage Mutant Ninja Turtles

The famous 1980s phenom put pizza in print, on the small screen, and on the big. The yummy pie was the favorite food of its four title heroes, all named for famous Renaissance artists—Donatello, Michelangelo, Raphael, and Leonardo.

Quiz

Question: Which one of the following musical acts has a song about pizza?

A. System of a Down
B. Olson Twins
C. Jonas Brothers
D. Vandals
E. All of the above

Correct Answer: E. All of the above. When people love you as much as pizza, they're going to sing about it.

Pizza Brain

Yes, folks, there is a world record for the world's largest collection of pizza memorabilia and collectibles: Pizza Brain. The brainchild (pun intended, of course) of artist Brian Dwyer and Christoper Powell, it started as Philadelphia's first pizza-themed art show. And promptly grew out of control. Over 25 artists displayed their work at the local gallery, which showed Brian the depth of our fascination with pizza itself. He sought out more and more pizza-related material, from toys to memorabilia. He wanted to turn the show into an annual event. He accrued so much stuff that he ended up opening a museum, Pizza Brain. The name is a play on Brian's first name (as you can see) which was his artistic alias. Headquartered in the Kensington neighborhood of Philadelphia, United States, the museum is also a restaurant with its flagship location on Frankford Avenue.

In August 2012, *Time* Magazine profiled Pizza Brain online after the museum claimed the *Guinness Book of World Records* title for the largest collection of pizza memorabilia in the world. A month later, Pizza Brain opened its doors to the public. The collection ranges from the familiar (toys, puzzles, magazine ads, comic books, etc.) to the absurd—including a stainless-steel pizza cutter shaped like the USS Enterprise, a Teenage Mutant Ninja Turtles Pizza Drop plinko arcade game circa 1990, an original Spanish poster print of the film *Do the Right Thing*, a copy of the John C. Holmes adult film *Hot and Saucy Pizza Girls*, and more than 150 vinyl 45s and LPs honoring pizza in song and lyric.

The posse at Pizza Brain showing off some of their favorite memorabilia.
Photo courtesy of Philadelphia Generocity.org

Tonight's Forecast: Dough with Widely Scattered Cheese

During the TV news, pizza is ordered during the weather more than than any other segment. No, I don't know why either.

Pizza Beer? Really?

Working out of their home brewery, Tom and Athena Seefurth used surplus tomatoes and garlic to create Mama Mia's Pizza Beer in 2006. It's in distribution and available online.

Totally Pizza

Cool, Fun, and Weird Pizzeria Names

Pizzeria owners all over the world get creative with business names. Here are just some of the domestic ones I've come across:

Maka Mia Pizza in Parkersburg, WV

A Slice of Vegas in Las Vegas, NV

Slice Slice Baby in Cincinnati, OH

F*cking Good Pizza in Northridge, CA

Lit Pizza in Baton Rouge, LA

Another One Bites the Crust in Fort Myers, FL

Gagglio's in Cuyahoga Falls, OH

Pizzaahhh! in Skokie, IL

Cheesus Crust in Seattle, WA

PizzaDoodle in Denver, CO

Peace a Pizza Boca Raton, FL

Circle in the Square Pizza Asheville, NC

Tennessy Willems Wood Oven Pizza in Ottawa, Canada

Ta-Boo Restaurant Palm Beach, FL

Upper Crust Pizza in Las Vegas, NV

Pizza My Dear in Las Vegas, NV

Pie in the Sky in Las Vegas, NV

Spaghetti Western in Pahrump, NV

Peter Piper Pizza in Roswell, NM

Roadrunner Pizza in Las Cruces, NM

Fox's Pizza Den in Las Cruces, NM

Pizza Orgasmica & Brewing Company in San Francisco, CA

Escape from New York Pizza in San Francisco, CA

Pudge Brothers Pizza in Seattle, WA

The Moose's Tooth in Anchorage, AK

King of New York Pizzeria in Los Angeles, CA

Pie-Casso in Stow, VT

Some Guys Pizza in Indianapolis, IN

Don't Make Me Turn This Pizzeria Around...

In 2012, Grand Central Pizza in Atlanta started banning unruly kids from the premises. The owner tacked a notice on the bottom of the menu that asks parents to remove their kids if the rugrats are causing a scene. The reason why? Bad reviews online from diners cited misbehaving kids as ruining their meals at the place.

Totally Pizza

Pizza Tycoon

This was a business simulator video game designed by the German company Software 2000 in 1994. It was published under the title Pizza Connection in Germany and as Pizza Tycoon by MicroProse abroad. The game was centered around being the manager of a pizza restaurant. Players chose from more than thirty different characters, created their own pizza, held cooking contests, and could tweak their virtual pizza joint's decor. You also had the ability to call upon local Mafia to sabotage competitors' restaurants or get money from criminal activities such as weapon and drug dealing. It was a cartoony game with a sense of humor. Two sequels followed: Fast Food Tycoon/Pizza Syndicate and Fast Food Tycoon 2/Pizza Connection 2.

App-tly Named

App game websites like Playpink.com even offer a ton of downloadable pizza games to boot. The girl-centric game site carries 63 games targeted at young 'uns. Among the titles: Pizza Passion, Pizza Roll, Divine Pizza, Pizza Truck, Lilly is a Pizza Maker, and plenty more.

EverQuest II

Somewhere, there's a game designer who's earned his or her place in Geek Heaven in one brilliant stroke: in-game pizza delivery. In February 2005, game developers added a pizza delivery system for EverQuest II players. By typing "/pizza," players were linked directly to the Pizza Hut ordering site without having to waste the five to ten seconds it takes to minimize the screen and navigate there on their own. This was the first time that a MMORPG (Massive Multi-player Online Role Playing Game) could accept orders for real world items.

Famous (And Not-So-Famous) Pizza Quotes

Everybody talks about pizza. From athletes to politicians, look around and you'll find great quotes from a ton of backgrounds. It's serious testimony to just how much this Italian import has suffused into every pore of world culture since it first immigrated to the United States more than a century ago.

"And I don't cook, either. Not as long as they still deliver pizza." —Tiger Woods

"A world devoid of tomato soup, tomato sauce, tomato ketchup and tomato paste is hard to visualize. Could the tin and processed food industries have got where they have without the benefit of the tomato compounds which colour, flavour, thicken and

Totally Pizza

conceal so many deficiencies? How did the Italians eat spaghetti before the advent of the tomato? Was there such a thing as tomato-less Neapolitan pizza?" —Elizabeth David, food author

"It's just like ordering a pizza." —Colin Farrell, actor, about calling out for prostitutes

"You better cut the pizza in four pieces because I'm not hungry enough to eat six." —Yogi Berra, MLB coach

"Without question, the greatest invention in the history of mankind is beer. Oh, I grant you that the wheel was also a fine invention, but the wheel does not go nearly as well with pizza." —Dave Barry, writer

"Sex and pizza, they say, are similar. When it's good, it's good. When it's bad, you get it on your shirt." —Mike Birbiglia, comedian

"I love my pizza so much, in fact, that I have come to believe in my delirium that my pizza might actually love me, in return. I am having a relationship with this pizza, almost an affair." —Elizabeth Gilbert, author

"Las Vegas is Everyman's cut-rate Babylon. Not far away there is, or was, a roadside lunch counter and over it a sign proclaiming in three words that a Roman emperor's orgy is now a democratic institution... "Topless Pizza Lunch." —Alistair Cooke

"Believe it or not, Americans eat 75 acres of pizza a day." —Boyd Matson, former anchor newscaster for *National Geographic* Explorer

"Pizza Hut Park is clearly becoming a major destination for marquee soccer events in the United States. The tremendous support by the entire soccer community in North Texas for MLS Cup 2005 makes Pizza Hut Park—one of the premier soccer complexes in the world—the perfect choice." —Don Garber, American commissioner of Major League Soccer

"There's no better feeling in the world than a warm pizza box on your lap." —Kevin James, actor and comedian

"Recognition is another important element of empowerment. Employees who make

Totally Pizza

empowered decisions should be recognized and rewarded. Celebrate them. Feature them in the company publication. Give them a prime parking spot near the front door for a week. Throw a pizza party. By doing so, you are sending a message to the rest of the workforce that empowerment is important." —John Tschohl, author and customer service guru

"There's a pizza place near where I live that sells only slices. In the back you can see a guy tossing a triangle in the air." —Steven Wright, stand up comedian

"Any time you have large numbers of people together and the TVis on, pizza works because it's so easy to share." —Jeremy White, editor-in-chief, *Pizza Today*

"Gourmet pizza is definitely a trend."—Jeremy White, editor-in-chief, *Pizza Today*

"If I were an Al Qaeda guy, I wouldn't go out for a pizza." —Lt. Col. Bryan Hilferty

"When Domino's Pizza approached M5 Industries and asked us to design and build the Steak Fanatic Pizza Couch, I knew it was something we wanted to be part of. The Steak Fanatic Pizza Couch is like a guy's dream come true—only the coolest gadgets and Domino's Pizza all within arm's reach." —Jamie Hyneman, star of MythBusters

"I do love Italian food. Any kind of pasta or pizza. My new pig out food is Indian food. I eat Indian food like three times a week. It's so good." —Jennifer Love Hewitt

"Up here in Seattle...you can walk into a mom-and-pop place and get a great pizza, but everyone in there has purple hair and nose rings." —Dwayne Northrop, CEO, Garlic Jim's Famous Gourmet Pizza

"It's very important, and if it's the child, no matter how prepubescent or ugly it is, you always say, 'Don't you look great?' You speak to the child even if the face is a pizza." —Joan Rivers, comedianne

"I didn't really see him. I just saw his pizza flipper as a blade, and I just saw that blade of the stick behind me so I dropped the pass. He was there, and he put it in." —Andrew Cogliano, NHL hockey player

"We're basically doing a feature film every week. This is big stuff. We blew up a

Totally Pizza

pizza kid, robbed a moving train, went down into the sewers, robbed a bank, did a chase scene with helicopters over downtown L.A....and that's just in the pilot!" —Mark Cullen, writer

"From my friend Wolfgang Puck to Ciro, when it comes to pizza, good taste can come from anything under the sun." —Bobby Flay, extremely famous chef

"You talk to anyone anywhere in the country, and they'll tell you about the pizzeria that they grew up with. The first pizza that you experience as a child becomes the pizza of your dreams and the pizza by which you judge all other pizza." —Ed Levine, New York food journalist

"I think I heard a few boos after I missed because they were going to miss out on their pizza, so I was definitely happy to see us get the next one." —Chris Phillips, NHL hockey player

"Now we're eating pizza as opposed to steak." —Arthur Miller, American playwright and essayist

"While they're here, make nice...Volunteer to show 'em the ropes. They won't know uptown from downtown. They've never ordered pizza by the slice. They don't know from alternate-side-of-the-street parking." —Ed Koch, former New York City mayor

"There's no more left in the wine cellar because all these Canadians are eating pizza and washing it down with Barolo." —Sergio Chiamparino, former mayor of Turin, Italy

"If you give a kid pizza, he might want a different kind of pizza. It might get worse." —Nick Collison, NBA basketball player

"People came up: 'I thought you were six feet tall.' I'm average height: five feet eight inches, skinny blonde. One guy says to me 'So, where's the fox from *Mystic Pizza*?'" —Julia Roberts

"Everyone is guilty at one time or another of throwing out questions that beg to be ignored, but mothers seem to have a market on the supply. "Do you want a spanking or do you want to go to bed?" "Don't you want to save some of the pizza for your brother?" "Wasn't there any change?" —Erma Bombeck, American humorist

Totally Pizza

"Pizza with pineapple, that's a cake... Pizza with cucumber, it's an insult." —Alessio Vinci, CNN journalist

"Hating the (New York) Yankees is as American as pizza pie, unwed mothers, and cheating on your income tax." —Mike Royko, journalist

"I love vegging out in front of the TV, eating pizza!" —Emma Bunton, British singer

"For the first time ever, overweight people outnumber average people in America. Doesn't that make overweight the average then? Last month you were fat, now you're average...hey, let's get a pizza!" —Jay Leno, comedian and talk show host

"Pizza is a lot like sex. When it's good, it's really good. When it's bad, it's still pretty good." —anonymous

"My idea of feng shui is to have them arrange the pepperoni in a circle on my pizza" —Charles Pierce

"When the moon hits your eye like a big pizza pie, that's amore" —from the song *That's Amore*, made famous by Dean Martin

"The perfect lover is one who turns into a pizza at 4:00 a.m." —Charles Pierce

"Today the whole world and especially the young are mad about pizzas and pizzerias. A consoling and significant fact: because there is always something so elementary, so clean and gay about a pizza, that it always gives me a rush of tenderness toward its addicts." —Sofia Loren, actress

"A good slice of pizza can be as good as a $200 meal in any restaurant." —Benicio Del Toro, actor

Appendix:
The Great Pizza Timeline

1st millennium BCE: According to archaeologists, this is where we have the first evidence of pizza's progenitor, flatbread, being made in Sardinia by the locals.

6th century BCE: Writings of Persian king Darius the Great mention his soldiers baking flatbread on their shields. This proto-pizza is covered with cheese and dates.

3rd century BCE: Famed Roman historian Marcus Porcius Cato's memoirs describe a "flat round of dough dressed with olive oil, herbs, and honey baked on stones."

1st century BCE: Virgil the famous Roman poet describes cakes or circles of pizza-esque bread in his most famous work, *The Aeneid*. In Pompeii and nearby Naples, a pizza predecessor is a common staple of the local cuisine. Modern archaeologists have plenty of evidence to prove that, thanks to the well-preserved Pompeiian ruins, where entire untouched kitchens, shops, and tools of the trade used for making and selling pizzas are found.

1522: Modern pizza is born in Naples after tomatoes are imported to Europe from the New World and are found to be tasty instead of poisonous. They're mated to bread products in what is perhaps the happiest marriage in history.

17th century: Pizza gains huge popularity in Naples among its citizens. Tourists? Not so much.

18th century: Queen Maria Carolina d'Asburgo Lorena of Naples supposedly has a special oven in her palace used for making pizzas. Some accounts attribute this to her kingly husband instead. Regardless, it's the earliest story of Naples' nobility taking an active interest in pizza.

Totally Pizza

1830: Pizza moves from street carts to the first dedicated pizzeria when Antica Pizzeria Port'Alba opens in Naples. By the end of the century, Neapolitans are eating pizza for breakfast, lunch, and dinner.

1889: King Umberto I of Italy and his wife Queen Margherita di Savoia have the most famous pizza chef in Naples, Raffaele Esposito, create three pizzas for them to sample. Whether or not this story is true, Pizza Margherita takes its name from the legend.

Late 19th and early 20th century: Italian immigrants move to the U.S in droves, bringing pizza with them. In Chicago, Italian street peddlers walk up and down Taylor Street selling hot slices of pizza. The pizza is kept in cylindrical drums with hot charcoal inside to maintain heat throughout the day.

1905: The first American business license for a pizzeria is granted to Gennaro Lombardi in New York City.

1910: Famous Joe's Tomato Pies pizzeria opens in Trenton's Chambersburg section.

1912: Papa's Tomato Pies, one of the oldest pizzerias that is still active, opens in Trenton's Chambersburg as well.

1924: Famous pizziaolo Anthony "Totonno'' Pero leaves Lombardi's to open his Totonno's Pizzeria in Coney Island, N.Y. Ettoire Boiardi immigrates to Cleveland from Italy and opens his restaurant, Giardino d'Italia. You and I know him better as Chef Boyardee.

1925: In New Haven, Connecticut, Frank Pepe opens his famous pizza joint, Frank Pepe Pizzeria Napoletana.

1943: Chicago deep-dish pizza is born when Ike Sewell and Rick Riccardo open Pizzeria Uno.

1945: Allied forces win World War II. American soldiers returning from the European Theater who've been to Italy bring home a taste for pizza, initiating its popularity outside of Little Italies in the United States.

Totally Pizza

1948: Frank Fiorillo produces the first successful pizza dough mix when he launches Roman Pizza Mix.

1954: World War II veteran Sherwood "Shakey" Johnson and Ben Plummer open the first Shakey's Pizza in Sacramento, California.

1956: Shakey's becomes the world's first pizza franchise when it opens a second location in Portland, Oregon.

1957: Celentano Brothers releases the world's first frozen pizza to supermarkets. Frozen pizzas and kits find a niche as a cheap way to for busy American parents to feed their kids.

1958: Frank Carnie, his brother Dan, and their friend John Bender found a little place called Pizza Hut in Wichita, KS.

1959: Mike and Marian Ilitch open the first Little Caesar's in Garden City, Michigan.

1960: Tom Monaghan and his brother James purchase "DomiNick's," a pizza store in Ypsilanti, Michigan. Monaghan borrowed $500 to buy the store.

1961: James Monaghan trades his half of DominiNick's to Tom for a Volkswagen Beetle.

1962: Pep and Ron Simek start selling pizza out of their tavern in Medford, Wisconsin. Located next to a cemetery, the place is named The Tombstone Tap and the name carries over to what becomes their frozen pizza business, Tombstone Pizza.

1965: Now sole owner of DomiNick's, Tom Monaghan renames his business "Domino's Pizza, Inc."

1967: The first Domino's Pizza franchise store opens in Ypsilanti, Michigan.

1968: Domino's company headquarters and commissary are destroyed by fire. The first Domino's store outside of Michigan opens in Burlington, Vermont.

1975: Amstar Corp., maker of Domino Sugar, institutes a trademark infringement lawsuit against Domino's Pizza.

Totally Pizza

1977: PepsiCo buys out Pizza Hut from founder Frank Carnie and the board for $300 million. Atari founder Nolan Bushnell opens the first Chuck E. Cheese's Pizza Time Theatre in San Jose, CA.

1978: Domino's reaches 200 stores. Nolan Bushnell leaves Atari and founds Pizza Time Theatre Inc.

1979: Pizza Hut introduces its Sicilian Pan Pizza. Units open in Kuwait and Abu Dhabi. Pizza Hut raises $342,000 for Easter Seals from national promotion. Bob Brock signs a co-development agreement with Bushnell to open approximately 280 Pizza Time Theatre stores across 16 states. Prior to opening his first franchise, Brock meets Aaron Fechter of Creative Engineering and decides to start his own company instead, ShowBiz. The Red Baron squadron takes to the skies at airshows. It's an aerial stunt team that promotes Red Baron Pizza.

1980: The world meets Pizza Hut's Pan Pizza. The chain opens its 4,000th store. Pizza Hut founder Frank Carney leaves the company and the pizza industry. The first ShowBiz Pizza Place opens in Kansas City, MO. Immediately a lawsuit is filed by Pizza Time Theatre against Brock for breach of contract. Brock immediately countersues. Alice Waters and Ed LaDou create what we now know as California pizza, independently of one another.

1981: Both Pizza Time Theatre and ShowBiz rapidly expand. Pizza Time Theatre becomes publicly traded.

1982: The Pizza Hut ET glass promotion is picked as the top marketing promotion of 1982 by the editorial staff of *Chain Marketing and Management*. Pizza Hut serves one and a half million pounds of pasta annually. In lawsuit land, a settlement is reached. ShowBiz agrees to pay Pizza Time Theatre a portion of its profits for 14 years (estimated to be valued at $50 million). Spago opens its doors with Ed LaDou as its pizza chef.

1983: Consumers on the go meet Pizza Hut's Personal Pan Pizza, with a five-minute guarantee. Pizza Hut celebrates its 25th anniversary. Pizza Hut employs 10,000 teenagers from 16 to 19 years old. Domino's first international store opens in Winnipeg, Canada. The 1,000th Domino's store opens. The first Domino's store opens on the Australian continent in Queensland. The Great Video Game Crash hits the United

Totally Pizza

States. Both Pizza Time Theatre and ShowBiz slow their expansions as sales begin to weaken for both chains.

1984: A young John Schnatter sells his prized 1972 Camaro and uses the proceeds to buy used restaurant equipment. His pizza business takes off leading to the birth of Papa John's. Pizza Hut's *Book It!* national reading incentive program is launched with 200,000 elementary students enrolled. There are now more pizza locations than hamburger restaurants in the United States. Pizzerias account for 9.9% of all restaurants in the United States. Bushnell resigns as chairman of Pizza Time Theatre. Shortly after that, the company is forced to file for Chapter 11 bankruptcy protection. Show-Biz begins the purchase of Pizza Time Theatre units and franchise rights.

1985: Pizza Hut launches its Priazzo and Calizza dishes. Domino's opens 954 units, for a total of 2,841, making Domino's the fastest-growing pizza company in the country. The first Domino's store opens in the United Kingdom, in Luten, England. The first Domino's store opens on the continent of Asia, in Minato, Japan. ShowBiz completes the merger of Pizza Time Theatre, obtaining their assets for cash and stock estimated at $35 million. The new company is renamed ShowBiz Pizza Time, Inc. and has 359 stores. Attorneys Rick Rosenfield and Larry Flax sire California Pizza Kitchen in Beverly Hills, California. Ed LaDou leads the charge by developing CPK's first pizza menu. In New York, the infamous Pizza Connection mafia trial begins. The first mega-trial of its kind, the historic case alleges 23 Mafiosi used independent pizzerias in the Mid-West and East Coast to smuggle and distribute over $1 billion in narcotics.

1986: Pizza Hut celebrates the opening of its 5,000th restaurant, located in Dallas, Texas. They also start delivering. The land speed record for fastest construction of a Pizza Hut restaurant takes place in Wichita, KS—39 days from start to finish (the national average is 85 days). With 272 stores, ShowBiz Pizza Time begins to show profits as financial restructuring is completed.

1987: ShowBiz Pizza Time opens its first new location in 3 years. New York's Pizza Connection trial concludes. Of the 23 Mafia defendants, 22 are convicted.

1988: The first Domino's store opens in South American, in Bogota, Columbia. Pizza Hut starts offering Hand-Tossed Traditional Pizza and celebrates its 30th anniversary with a total of more than 6,000 restaurants and delivery units worldwide. President Ronald Reagan awards a Private Initiative Citation to Pizza Hut President Art Gunther for the creation of the *Book It!* program.

Totally Pizza

1989: Domino's opens its 5,000th store and introduces Pan Pizza to its product line. It's the company's first new take on pizza. The Pizza Hut Jobs Plus program expands nationwide to employ more than 10,000 people with physical and developmental disabilities. The Jobs Plus program is recognized as the largest corporate initiative of its kind in the food service industry. Pizza Hut opens its 1,000th international unit in Welland, Ontario, Canada. Pizza Hut now serves 54 countries. On the movie marketing front, Pizza Hut sells 9.1 million "Land Before Time" puppets. When released to the public, the movie enjoyed the largest opening ever for an animated feature up until that time. For the first time in history, Pizza Hut pizza is delivered to the White House. First Lady Barbara Bush throws a party for 200 Washington, D.C. children during a "Reading is Fundamental" reception. Hopefully she shared the pizza with them.

1990: Domino's Pizza signs its 1,000th franchise. Pizza Hut system sales reach $4 billion. Pizza Hut delivers more than 1,340,000 pizzas on Super Bowl Sunday (about 7,000 pies a minute). Kamran Atri, assistant manager in Leesburg, VA serves his way into the *Guinness Book of World Records* by waiting tables at the Leesburg, VA Pizza Hut restaurant for 136 hours, donating $1,200 in tips to the Loudoun County Shelter for Abused Women & Children. More than 4,000 Jobs Plus employees work for Pizza Hut. Personal Pan Pizza becomes available at 1,000 Stop 'N Go convenience stores. A federal court rules that Domino's Pizza didn't infringe on the Domino Sugar trademark. Concept Unification is introduced at Pizza Time Theatres, removing the Rock-Afire Explosion from ShowBiz stores and replacing them with Chuck E. Cheese characters.

1992: Pizza Hut introduces a lunch buffet in 1,800 units. Pizza Hut sets up two mobile hot trailers in Florida City and Goulds, FL after Hurricane Andrew wreaks havoc. When all's said and done, the company has provided 120,000 free meals to relief volunteers and to those who lost their homes. Pizza Hut also redesigned its delivery boxes to save 275,000 trees a year. Domino's rolls out bread sticks, the company's first national non-pizza menu item. California Pizza Kitchen now has 26 locations. PepsiCo shells out nearly $100 million for 67 percent of the chain. Flax and Rosenfield each receive $17.5 million. The purchase amount is thought to be more than CPK is worth, driving PepsiCo to hit the gas and expand CPK faster.

1993: Pizza Hut introduces Bigfoot Pizza—two square feet of pizza cut into 21 slices. It also launches The Harvest Program nationwide to donate surplus food to food rescue agencies. Pizza Hut makes its fastest and farthest delivery: 600 large pepperoni

Totally Pizza

pizzas on a 24-hour flight from Dover Air Force Base to U.S. service personnel in Mogadishu, Somalia. Pizza Hut also sets a new company records for sales and profits. In September, Pizza Hut introduces Chunky Style Pizza. Finally, the company signs contracts with 30 hotel companies throughout the United States to provide delivery service to their registered guests. Domino's rolls out Crunchy Thin Crust pizza nationwide. The company discontinues the 30-minute guarantee and re-emphasizes the Total Satisfaction Guarantee: If for any reason you are dissatisfied with your Domino's Pizza dining experience, they will re-make your pizza or refund your money.

1994: Pizza Hut becomes the single largest retailer of basketballs in the United States, selling 3.7 million balls during its NCAA Final Four promotion. (I'm pretty sure they didn't hold the title for long.) Pizza Hut's 9,700 square foot Super Pizza Hut restaurant and entertainment center debuts in Mexico City. In Beirut, Pizza Hut reopens after being closed during the Gulf War. Not to be outdone, soccer legend Pele kicks a ball through the door of Pizza Hut restaurant number 10,000 in Sao Paulo, Brazil on April 13. Domino's rolls out Buffalo Wings in all U.S. Stores. PepsiCo has added 43 CPK stores but cut corners by switching the company over to frozen vegetables and cheese. After throwing tens of millions of dollars into the expansion, PepsiCo is forced to slow it down. Flax and Rosenfield would later switch CPK back to fresh toppings. Papa John's scores a major win when Pizza Hut founder Frank Carney returns to the industry as a Papa John's franchisee. In Arizona, artisan pizzaiolo Chris Bianco opens up Pizzeria Bianco, which is now one of the most famous artisan pizzerias in America.

1995: Domino's Pizza International division opens its 1,000th store. The chain's first store in Africa opens up in Cairo, Egypt. Pizza Hut launches the "You'll Love The Stuff We're Made Of" campaign. Buffalo Wings make it onto the Pizza Hut menu. Pizza Hut launches Pizzeria Stuffed Crust Pizza, which immediately sets company sales records and customer obesity records. The *Deliver Me Home* program is created by Pizza Hut with the National Center for Missing and Exploited Children. It is tested at the Dallas/Fort Worth International Airport to inform the community of an important identification tool in helping to locate, identify and return missing children to their families. Pizza Hut wins the 1995 "Choice of Chains" award for Best Pizza Chain sponsored annually by *Restaurants & Institutions* magazine, making Pizza Hut the "Best Pizza Chain" ten of the last eleven years. Tombstone Pizza unveils a revolutionary self-rising frozen pizza crust that really raises the bar on what's possible with frozen pizza.

Totally Pizza

1996: Domino's launches its website on the Internet and rolls out flavored crusts in limited-time-only promotions nationally for the first time. The company reaches record sales of $2.8 billion system-wide. Pizza Hut airs its first ever ad during the Super Bowl. Meanwhile, its drivers deliver 30% of the 12 million pizzas ordered on Super Bowl Sunday. This is the biggest pizza delivery day of the year. On May 30, the world is introduced to Pizza Hut's Italian Chicken and Chicken Supreme poultry-topped pies.

1997: Pizza Hut launches "Totally New Pizzas" a quality initiative putting sliced, fresh vegetables and meaty meats on pizzas. Part of the topping makeover includes a meatier pepperoni. This year also sees the launch of "The Edge Pizza" from Pizza Hut. Domino's Pizza opens its 1,500th store outside of the United States, opening seven stores in one day on five continents consecutively. Domino's Pizza launches a campaign to update the company logo and store interiors with brighter colors and a newer look. Papa John's gives Pizza Hut a big middle finger by running TV ads featuring Frank Carney saying, "Sorry, guys, I found a better pizza." to a room full of faux Pizza Hut execs. Pizza Hut counters with a huge lawsuit against Papa John's over its advertising. Meanwhile at California Pizza Kitchen, private equity firm Bruckmann, Rosser, Sherrill & Company buys out PepsiCo's two-thirds stake, intending to take CPK public in 2000.

1998: Pizza Hut turns 40. Unlike some people who celebrate their 40th with a Corvette, blue pills, and a twenty-year-old girlfriend, Pizza Hut linstead launches "The Sicilian Pizza." It features a crust with garlic, basil and oregano baked right into it. Pizza Hut also starts its "The Best Pizzas Under One Roof" campaign and features Sony's Crash Bandicoot in the Stuffed Crust Pizza/Sony Promotion. Domino's launches its innovative Domino's HeatWave—a hot bag using patented technology that keeps pizza oven-hot to the customer's door. Domino's Pizza opens a 6,000th store in San Francisco, California. Domino's Pizza founder, Tom Monaghan, announces retirement and sells 93% of his company to Bain Capital, Inc. Yes, THAT Bain Capital, Inc. ShowBiz Pizza Time changes its name to Chuck E. Cheese Entertainment Inc.

1999: Pizza Hut launches The Big New Yorker Pizza. It's a 16-inch pizza with a sweeter, savory sauce and 100% real cheese, cut into 8 big foldable slices. The ad campaign for the Big New Yorker features Fran Drescher, Spike Lee and Donald Trump. The celebrity campaign launched in the pre-game advertising for Super Bowl XXXIII. Pizza Hut also introduces Pizza PlayStuff, a kid's program that enables customers to purchase the featured kids' toy for $.99 with any pizza purchase. Pizza Hut, KFC and Taco Bell are the exclusive global restaurant partners for *Star Wars Episode I: The Phantom Menace*. This is the first time that all three brands unite under one theme. It's also the first time George Lucas disappoints millions of old school Star Wars fans. Sadly, it won't be the last. David Brandon is named Chairman and Chief Executive Officer of Domino's Pizza. Domino's Pizza announces record worldwide sales results exceeding $3.36 billion for 1999. .

2000: Domino's Pizza International opens its 2,000th store outside the United States. Domino's Pizza celebrates 40 years of delivering pizza and innovation to homes around the world. During the past four decades, Domino's has paved the way for businesses involved in food delivery, employing practices that have set the standard in the industry. Domino's Pizza announces record sales results exceeding $3.54 billion for 2000. Pizza Hut becomes the first company in history to place its logo on the world's largest proton rocket. The space sponsorship campaign is part of the company's dramatic turnaround and re-imaging campaign, which included a more than $500 million investment over five years to modernize and upgrade Pizza Hut units around the globe.

2001: Pizza Hut and ad agency BBDO create a national television commercial in 24 hours about the Bush-Gore election, in which no winner was determined after election night. Pizza Hut also becomes the first company in history to deliver pizza to the pioneers living in outer space on the International Space Station (ISS). The creation and delivery of the world's first space-consumable pizza is the culmination of nearly a year of collaboration between Pizza Hut and Russian food scientists. Domino's introduces one of the most bizarre new products in the company's history—CinnaStix. Domino's 7,000th store opens in Brooklyn, NY. Domino's launches two-year national partnership with the Make-A-Wish Foundation of America. Domino's stores in New York City and Washington DC provide more than 12,000 pizzas to relief workers at Ground Zero following the September 11 tragedy. Domino's Pizza International division establishes Domino's first regional resource center with the majority stake purchase of a franchise in The Netherlands, setting the stage for expansion on the European continent.

2002: In February 2002, Domino's Pizza acquired 82 franchised stores in the Phoenix, Arizona, market, making it the largest store acquisition in the company's history.

Totally Pizza

2003: Domino's announces a multi-year partnership with the National Association for Stock Car Auto Racing (NASCAR) and becomes the "Official Pizza of NASCAR." Domino's is named Chain of the Year by *Pizza Today* magazine, a leading pizza trade publication. Domino's combines two culinary classics – pizza and Philadelphia cheese steak – to create the all-new Domino's Philly Cheese Steak Pizza. Rosenfield and Flax re-take control of California Pizza Kitchen in the wake of erroneous earnings numbers reported by the previous leadership.

2004: Domino's launches Domino's Cheesy Dots, round balls of dough covered in a blend of zesty melted cheeses. Domino's becomes an associate sponsor for the Drive for Diversity program, a minority driver development program designed to provide a steady pipeline of well-trained and supported minority drivers for the NASCAR circuit. Domino's Pizza, Inc. begins trading common stock on the New York Stock Exchange (NYSE) in July 2004, under the new ticker symbol "DPZ." The company announces a three-year partnership with St. Jude Children's Research Hospital. In September, the Domino's Doublemelt Pizza is launched nationwide.

2005: Domino's Pizza celebrates the completion of the three-year renovation of its World Resource Center in Ann Arbor, Mich. The renovation marks the first major improvement to the company's world headquarters since Domino's founder Tom Monaghan opened the sprawling Domino's Farms. Domino's Pizza Australia and Domino's UK open their 400th stores in Aspley, Brisbane. Domino's Pizza efforts worldwide raise $220,000 to support southeast Asia tsunami relief efforts. Domino's Pizza launches its American Classic Cheeseburger Pizza in conjunction with its appearance as a featured task on the NBC hit reality show, "The Apprentice." The 500th Chuck E. Cheese location is opened. As part of the yearly Smithsonian Folklife Festival, the Smithsonian Institute invites Ed LaDou to demo his pizza techniques at the event.

2006: Domino's celebrates the opening of its 8,000th store with simultaneous celebrations of the opening of its 5,000th U.S. store in Huntley, Illinois, and its 3,000th international store in Panama City, Panama.

2007: Domino's introduces Oreo Dessert Pizza—a thin dessert-style crust that's layered with vanilla sauce and covered with Oreo cookie crumbles and then topped with sweet icing. Domino's introduces its Veterans and Delivering the Dream franchising programs. The company also rolls out online and mobile ordering, much to the hap-

Totally Pizza

piness of gamer geeks worldwide. Domino's is ranked in the Top 10 for the ninth time in *Entrepreneur* magazine's annual listing of great franchise opportunities. Gourmet pizza innovator Ed LaDou dies of cancer in Santa Monica, California. In the wake of a fatal accident, Red Baron retires its Flying Squadron.

2008: Dominos launches the Pizza Tracker technology that allows you to track your order from start to finish online. Papa John's now has more than 3,300 locations in all 50 states plus more than 30 countries.

2009: The European Union establishes a ruling that protects Naples' Neapolitan pizza as a cultural heritage food. All pizzerias that want to create real Neapolitan pizza must comply with the strict standards for ingredients and processes of its preparation.

2012: Papa John's is targeted with a class action suit alleging it sent more than 500,000 unwanted text messages to customers.

Bibliography

Alexander, Shana. *The Pizza Connection: Lawyers, Money, Drugs, Mafia*. Grove Press, 1988.

Anderson, Burton. *Treasures of the Italian Table*. William Morrow, 1994.

Anon. "Amstar Corporation, Plaintiff-Appellee, v. Domino's Pizza, Inc. and Atlanta Pizza, Inc., Pizza Enterprises, Inc. and Pizza Services, Inc., Hanna Creative Enterprises, Inc., Defendants-Appellants". *United States Court of Appeals for the Fifth Circuit*, May 2, 1980.

Anon. "Company History." *Chuck E. Cheese Official Site. CEC Entertainment, Inc.*

Anon. "First North Korean Pizzeria Opens." BBC News, March 16, 2009, http://news.bbc.co.uk/2/hi/asia-pacific/7945816.stm.

Anon. "Found: Papa John's Long-Lost Camaro! Kentucky Man Receives $250,000 Finder's Fee." *Papa John's*, August 25, 2009, https://ir.papajohns.com/news-releases/news-release-details/found-papa-johns-long-lost-camaro-kentucky-man-receives-250000?ReleaseID=404954.

Anon. "Hotbags: Turning Up the Heat on Deliveries." *PMQ (Pizza Magazine Quarterly)*, Winter 2002.

Anon. "Pizza Time." *The Sacramento Bee*, December 2, 1979. p. 93.

Anon. "Red Baron Pizza Biplane Squadron to Retire." *Associated Press*. December 3, 2007.

"Sammy's Woodfired Pizza." Sammyspizza.com, *https://sammyspizza.com/company*.

"2 Kids Left Behind at 2 Different Chuck E. Cheese's." ABC News, https://abcnews.go.com/GMA/video/kids-left-chuck-cheeses-forgotten-children-restaurant-15900805.

"About Us." *Associazione Vera Pizza Napoletana*, https://americas.pizzanapoletana.org/en/.

Anon. "Annie's Organic-Rising Crust Pizza." *Refrigerated & Frozen Foods*, March 26, 2012.

"Consumer Trend Reports: Pizza." *Technomic*, https://www.technomic.com/reports/consumer/consumer-trend-reports/pizza.

Totally Pizza

Anon. "Das sind die besten deutschen Computerspiele." Welt.de, 1994, https://www.welt.de/spiele/gallery120615650/Das-sind-die-besten-deutschen-Computerspiele.html.

Anon. "Eagle Boys Takes Aim at Rivals." *Adnews*, November 30, 2007.

"International Pizza Expo and Conference." *Pizza Today*. https://pizzaexpo.pizzatoday.com/.

Anon. "Papa Murphy's International, Inc. History." *International Directory of Company Histories*, Vol. 54. St. James Press, 2003.

Anon. "Pizzeria Owner Dumped Mice on Rivals, Cops Say." CBS News, March 1, 2011, https://www.cbsnews.com/news/pizzeria-owner-dumped-mice-on-rivals-cops-say/.

"Restaurant Bans Crying Kids: Grant Central Pizza of Atlanta, Ga. Restaurant, Enacts New Rule." *HuffPost*, February 21, 2012, https://www.huffpost.com/entry/grant-central-georgia-crying-kids_n_1291446.

Anon. "Rivals take pizza fight to "Apprentice'." *Tampa Bay Times*, August 25, 2005.

Anon. "Size Matters in Pizza Punch-Up." *News Limited*, December 10, 2007.

Anon. "Tombstone Pizza Corporation History." *International Directory of Company Histories*, Vol. 13. St. James Press, 1996.

Anon. "A History of Detroit-Style Pizza and Where to Find It." *Pure Michigan*, https://www.michigan.org/article/trip-idea/history-of-detroit-style-pizza-where-to-find-it.

Baer, Drake. "This Marketing Insight Made Papa John's A Household Name." *Business Insider*, May 21, 2014. https://www.businessinsider.com/papa-johns-marketing-insight-2014-5?IR=T/.

Berry, Marc; Penenberg, Adam. *Spooked: Espionage in Corporate America*. Basic Books, 2008.

Betzold, Michael. "Domino's Can't Avoid Mr. Noid." *Detroit Free Press, February 1, 1989*.

Botts, Marc S. "Guru of Gourmet: Pizza Innovator Still has Tricks Up his Sleeve." *Pizza Today*, July 5, 2005. https://web.archive.org/web/20080502053051/http://www.pizzatoday.com/features_articles.shtml?article=MTI1MXN1cGVyMTI0OHNlY3JldDEyNTU.

Boyer, Peter J. "The Deliverer - A Pizza Mogul Funds a Moral Crusade." *The New Yorker*, February 19, 2007.

Brack, Ray. "Shakey's Serving Music with Pizza". *Billboard*, October 7, 1967.

Brownlee, John. "Death And Pizza: How Domino's Lost Its Mascot". *Co.Design*, July 10,

Totally Pizza

2014, https://www.fastcompany.com/3032911/kidnapping-death-pizza-how-dominos-lost-its-mascot.

Brush, Mark. "Domino's Pizza Renews Commitment to Ann Arbor". *Michigan Radio*, October 22, 2012.

Burros, Marian. "Alice Waters: Food Revolutionary." *The New York Times*, August 14, 1996.

Capuzzo, Jill. "Trenton Tomato Pies Are Still A Staple of the New Jersey Pizza Scene." *New Jersey Monthly*, January 12, 2010.

Carbone, Nick. "Pizza Crusade: Domino's Managers Charged With Burning Down Rival Papa John's Store." *Time.com*, October 30, 2011.

Chappell, Bill. "Cheese-Smuggling Ring Is Brought Down in Canada." *NPR*, September 27, 2012.

Chaudhry, Rajan. "McPizza? McDonald's widens pizza test: pizza operators gird for assault." *Nation's Restaurant News*, July 31, 1989.

Child, Julia. *Mastering the Art of French Cooking Vol. 1*. Alfred A. Knopf, New York, 1961.

Christenson, Bridget. "How Totino's Got its Start." Taste of General Mills, December 11, 2014, https://blog.generalmills.com/2014/12/how-totinos-got-its-start/

Chu, Louisa. "Family's Stuffed-Pizza Dynasty Began with a Fight." *Chicago Tribune*, September 19, 2016.

Collins, Glen. "Metropolitan Diary." *The New York Times*, June 18, 1980, C2.

Conway, Lawrence. "New York restaurant serving up $1,000 PIZZA... decadent dish is topped with two of the world's top caviars." *Daily Mail*, June 18, 2012, https://www.dailymail.co.uk/news/article-2161007/Ninos-Bellissima-Pizza-New-York-restaurant-serves-1k-PIZZA-2-caviars.html.

Coomes , Steeve. "Who's Who: Ed LaDou." *Pizza Marketplace*, August 29, 2003, https://web.archive.org/web/20071011075621/http://www.pizzamarketplace.com/article.php?id=2653.

D'Oro, Rachel. "The Men Behind the Machine." *Brokentoothbrewing.net*, December 1, 1998, http://brokentoothbrewing.net/about/.

Dalby, Andrew. *Food in the ancient world from A to Z*. London, New York: Routledge, 2003.

Daniels, Calvin. "Learning Farming Via the Pizza." *SaskToday*, June 10, 2015, https://www.sasktoday.ca/central/agriculture/learning-farming-via-the-pizza-4076667.

Totally Pizza

Efron, Lauren. "Chuck E. Cheese: Where Family Feuds at Birthday Parties Turn into Violent Brawls." *ABC News*, February 27, 2012, https://abcnews.go.com/US/chuck-cheese-family-feuds-birthday-parties-turn-violent/story?id=15803726.

Fimrite, Peter. "Pizza Trail Betrays Car Thieves / Police arrest 9 teens in Honda-hungry East Bay ring." *SFGate*, October 9, 1996, https://www.sfgate.com/crime/article/Pizza-Trail-Betrays-Car-Thieves-Police-arrest-9-2963370.php.

Flathers, Harley. "Back and Forth: Shakey's Pizza was the Place to Be." *PostBulletin.com*, January 23, 2014.

Freeman, Mike. "Pizza and crime? The Pizza Flyer Bill, Now on the Books, Targets Organized Crime Rings that Scam Hotel Guests." *Freeline Media Orlando*, June 16, 2011, https://freelinemediaorlando.com/pizza-and-crime-the-pizza-flyer-bill-now-on-the-books-targets-organized-crime-rings-that-scam-hotel-guests/2571/.

Galloway, Paul. "A Half-baked Story on How Deep-Dish Pizza was Created in Chicago." *Chicago Tribune*, January 8, 1986.

Goldberg, Marty and Vendel, Curt. *Atari Inc: Business is Fun*. Syzygy Press, 2012.

Hamacher, Brian. "Domino's Pizza Managers Charged With Burning Down Papa John's." *NBC Miami*, October 31, 2011, https://www.nbcmiami.com/news/local/dominos-pizza-managers-charged-with-burning-down-papa-johns/2057666/.

Helstosky, Carol F. *Garlic and Oil: Food and Politics in Italy*. Berg Publishers, 2004.

Helstosky, Carol. *Pizza: A Global History*. Reaktion Books, 2008.

Pollack, Penny and Ruby, Jeffrey Michael. *Everybody Loves Pizza: The Deep Dish on America's Favorite Food*. Clerisy Press, 2005.

Levine, Ed. *Pizza: A Slice of Heaven: The Ultimate Pizza Guide and Companion*. Universe, 2005.

Hesling, Johanna. "Pizza Enthusiast Sets New Memorabilia World Record". *Guinness World Records*, August 3, 2011, https://www.guinnessworldrecords.com/news/pizza-enthusiast-sets-new-memorabilia-world-record/.

Higgins, Chris. "6 Obscure Facts About the Noid." *Mental Floss*, June 26, 2015, https://www.mentalfloss.com/article/18769/6-obscure-facts-about-noid.

Holbert, Ginny. "The Wright price—Monaghan's Deals Raise Stakes" *Chicago Sun Times*, April, 1990.

https://newsfeed.time.com/2011/10/30/pizza-crusade-dominos-managers-charged-with-burning-down-rival-papa-johns-store/.

Totally Pizza

https://web.archive.org/web/20150228152405/http:/www.news.com.au/national/size-matters-in-pizza-punch-up/story-e6frfkp9-1111115077983.

https://www.adnews.com.au/DB767BE9-0FB9-4A48-AEE46E58B12A90F0.

https://www.npr.org/sections/thetwo-way/2012/09/27/161917296/cheese-smuggling-ring-is-brought-down-in-canda.

https://www.nytimes.com/2004/05/02/business/openers-the-goods-how-frozen-pizza-got-hot.html.

https://www.refrigeratedfrozenfood.com/articles/86147-annie-s-organic-rising-crust-pizza
https://www.tampabay.com/archive/2005/04/06/rivals-take-pizza-fight-to-apprentice/.

Ipri, Dana Shay. "Pizza, Bagels and 'Brooklynized' Water — Oh My!" *Forward.com*, October 26, 10, https://forward.com/schmooze/132512/pizza-bagels-and-brooklynized-water-oh-my/.

Jackson, Kenneth T.; Keller, Lisa; Flood, Nancy. *The Encyclopedia of New York City (2nd ed.).* New Haven: Yale University Press, 2010.

Jacob, Jeanne; Ashkenazi, Michael. *The World Cookbook: The Greatest Recipes from Around the Globe, 2nd Edition [4 Volumes]: The Greatest Recipes from Around the Globe.* ABC-CLIO January 15, 2014. 806.

James Leonard, *Living the Faith: A Life of Tom Monaghan.* University of Michigan Press, 2012.

John Marzulli. "Mob sauce summit! Colombos and Bonannos had Sitdown over Suspected Family Recipe Theft from L&B Spumoni Gardens." *New York Daily News*, June 3, 2012, https://www.nydailynews.com/new-york/mob-sauce-summit-colombos-bonannos-sitdown-suspected-family-recipe-theft-b-spumoni-gardens-article-1.1095311.

Johnson, Greg. "Taco Bell's Parent to Be Based in Louisville, Ky." *Los Angeles Times*, August 1, 1997.

Johnson, Greg; Maharaj, Davan. "2 Rival CEOs Have More in Common Than Usual." *Los Angeles Times*, April 4, 2000.

K, Jul. "Pizza Time's Vaudeville Theatre." *Western Foodservice*, March 1979.

Kent, Steve L. *The Ultimate History of Video Games: From Pong to Pokémon and Beyond: The Story behind the Craze That Touched Our Lives and Changed the World.* Roseville, CA: Prima Pub., 2001.

Kent, Steve L. *The Ultimate History of Video Games: From Pong to Pokémon and Beyond: The Story behind the Craze That Touched Our Lives and Changed the World.* Prima Pub., 2001.

Totally Pizza

Khatri, Taz. "Local Food." *YouTube*, July 3, 2009 https://www.youtube.com/watch?v=_rJxWXKk-mw.

Kinkead, Gwen. "High Profits from a Weird Pizza Combination." *Fortune*, July 1982. 62–68.

Koehner, Brendan. "Openers: The Goods; How Frozen Pizza Got Hot." *New York Times*, May 2, 2004.

Kretzmann, David. "How Domino's Is Poised to Benefit From India." *Fool.com*, December 21, 2013, https://www.fool.com/investing/general/2013/12/21/how-dominos-is-poised-to-benefit-from-india.aspx.

Kwitny, Johnathan. *Vicious Circles: The Mafia in the Marketplace*. W. W. Norton & Company, 1981.

Lacter, Mark. "Second Helping: How the two guys who founded California Pizza Kitchen kept their unlikely partnership—and their company—alive." *Los Angeles Magazine*, August 2008.

Lauriston, Robert. "Pizza Smackdown: SoCal Chain Goes Head to Head with Hometown Favorite." *San Francisco Weekly*, September 26, 2007.

Lemire, Jonathan. "Bronx pizza parlor delivering calzones - and cocaine, say Feds." *New York Daily News*, April 2, 2009, https://www.nydailynews.com/news/crime/bronx-pizza-parlor-delivering-calzones-cocaine-feds-article-1.359526.

Levine, E. "The Road to Pizza Nirvana Goes Through Phoenix." *The New York Times*, July 7, 2004.

Levine, Ed. *Serious Eats: A Comprehensive Guide to Making & Eating Delicious Food Wherever You Are*. Random House Digital, Inc, 2011. pp. 99–100.

Liwag Dixon, Christine-Marie. "The Untold Truth of Pizza Hut." *Mashed*, August 18, 2017, https://www.mashed.com/81172/untold-truth-pizza-hut/

Mace, Scott. "Rat Dishes Up Pizza, Computerized Entertainment". *Infoworld*, December 21, 1981.

Madrigal, Alexis C. "Chuck E. Cheese's, Silicon Valley Startup: The Origins of the Best Pizza Chain Ever." *The Atlantic*. July 17, 2013.

Madrigal, Alexis. "The 3 Big Advances in the Technology of the Pizza Box". The Atlantic, July 18, 2011.

Mama Mia Pizza Beer, "Main Page." *Mama Mia Pizza Beer*, https://www.mammamiapizzabeer.com/main.php

Totally Pizza

Marcus, Erica. "Grandma Pizza: the Full Story." *Newsday*, September 10, 2008, https://www.newsday.com/lifestyle/restaurants/grandma-pizza-the-full-story-1.825269.

Meyer, Zlati. *"Domino's Farms' Tom Monaghan Granted Temporary Order Halting Contraceptive Coverage." Detroit Free Press, December 31, 2012.*

Mikkelson, David. "FBI Orders 19 Pizzas Delivered to Psychiatric Hospital?." *Snopes*, August 24, 2000, https://www.snopes.com/fact-check/pizza-spy/

Millman, Nancy. "Pepsico To Spin Off Restaurants." *Chicago Tribune,* January 24, 1997.

Mitgang, Herbert. "Pizza a la Mode." *New York Times*, February 12, 1956.

Morris, Kieran. "A Brief History of Socca, France's Chickpea Pancake." *Culture Trip*, February 6, 2020, https://theculturetrip.com/europe/france/articles/a-brief-history-of-socca-frances-chickpea-pancake/.

Moskin, Julia. "Pepperoni: America's Favorite Topping". *The New York Times*, February 1, 2011.

Neves, Regina (10 July 2007). "Capital da Pizza, Sabores para Todos." *Gazetta Mercantil*, July 10, 2007, http://indexet.gazetamercantil.com.br/arquivo/2007/07/10/330/Capital-da-pizza,-sabores-para-todos.html.

Nilsson, Magnus. *The Nordic Cook Book*. London: Phaidon, 2015. 476.

Nino's Restaurant. "About Nino's." *Nino's Restaurant*, https://www.ninosnyc.com/about.

Northrup, Laura. "Dominos Accidentally Gives Away 11,000 Pizzas in Bailout Promotion." *Consumerist*, April 1, 2009, https://consumerist.com/2009/04/01/dominos-accidentally-gives-away-11000-pizzas-in-bailout-promotion/.

Norway, Arthur Hamilton. *Naples: Past and Present*. Methuen & Co., London, 1905.

Oates, Sarah. "Chuck E. Cheese Gets New Lease on Life." *The Washington Post,* July 15, 1985.

Packer, Linda. "Catering To Kids." *Food Service Marketing*, October 1979. pp. 46–47.

Pennsylvania Crime Commission. *A Decade of Organized Crime*. Office of the Attorney General, Commonwealth of Pennsylvania, 1980.

Pierce, Charles P. "The Crusaders: A powerful faction of religious and political conservatives is waging a latter-day counterreformation, battling widespread efforts to liberalize the American Catholic Church. And it has the clout and the connections to succeed". *The Boston Globe*, November 2, 2003.

Pizza La. "Corporate Info." *Pizza-La*, https://www.pizza-la.co.jp/CorporateInfo.aspx.

Totally Pizza

Pous, Terri. "Slice of History: First Pizza Museum to Open in Philadelphia". *Time Newsfeed*, August 7, 2012, https://newsfeed.time.com/2012/08/07/slice-of-history-first-pizza-museum-to-open-in-philadelphia/.

Prewitt, Milford. "ShowBiz Parent Merges Concepts Into One Big Pie". *Nation's Restaurant News*, September 1, 1990.

Prior, Anna. "Calling All Cars: Trouble at Chuck E. Cheese's, Again." *Wall Street Journal*, December 9, 2008.

Proctor, Cathy Proctor and Sweeney, Patrick. "Denver's Big Cheese: Leprino Cuts a Huge Slice of the Mozzarella Market." *Denver Business Journal*, December 29, 2002.

Prud'Homme, Alex. "Taking the Gospel to the Rich". *The New York Times Company,* February 14, 1999.

Reid, Tim. "Yeltsin's Drunken Semi-Naked Pizza Hunt Revealed." *Independent.ie*, September 22, 2009, https://www.independent.ie/world-news/americas/yeltsins-drunken-semi-naked-pizza-hunt-revealed-26568066.html.

Reinhart, Peter. *American Pie: My Search for the Perfect Pizza*. Ten Speed Press, October 27, 2010, 58-61, 180.

Rhodes, Jesse. "Clarence Birdseye, the Man Behind Modern Frozen Food." *Smithsonian Magazine*, May 16, 2012, https://www.smithsonianmag.com/arts-culture/clarence-birdseye-the-man-behind-modern-frozen-food-95808503/.

Richman, Adam. *America the Edible: A Hungry History, from Sea to Dining Sea*. Rodale, 2010. 79–81.

Richman, Alan. "American Pie: The 25 Best Pizzas You'll Ever Eat." *GQ*, May, 2009.

Rigg, Sarah A; Ramey, Robert. "From Pizza to Philanthropy: a Conversation with Tom Monaghan at Domino's Farms." *mlive.com*.

Roberts, L. "Chris Bianco Surprises With New Trattoria and Pizzeria in Phoenix." *Serious Eats*, May 10, 2013, https://www.seriouseats.com/pizza-recipes-5117816.

Rose, J. "The Prince of Pizza: Chef Bianco's Pies are Best in the World." *The Arizona Republic*, June 21, 2006.

Rose, J. "Pizzeria Bianco Chef's Tips and Recipes in 'Martha Stewart Living'." *The Arizona Republic*, April 15, 2009.

Totally Pizza

Rosner, Helen. "The Pizza Stone, Brought to You By Pat Bruno And Julia Child." *Grub Street,* August 14, 2009, https://www.grubstreet.com/2009/08/the_pizza_stone_brought_to_you.html.

Scott-Uda, Mary "Breakfast in Naples." *The Century Magazine,* Vol. 62, May, 1901. *Shapiro, Bill; Bielski, Vince. "Domino's Pizza." Mother Jones,* March–April 1994.

Shapiro, Eben. "McDonald's Hopes Pizza Will Be the Next McHit." *New York Times,* September 20, 1989.

Shapiro, T. Rees. "Jeno Paulucci, Food Visionary Behind the Pizza Roll, Dies at 93". *Washington Post,* November 30, 2011.

Shrikant, Adit. "How Dipping Sauce for Pizza Became Oddly Necessary." *Eater,* July 27, 2017, https://www.eater.com/2017/7/27/16021832/pizza-dipping-sauce-papa-johns-garlic-dominos-sauce.

Sinclair, Charles G.. *International Dictionary of Food and Cooking.* Fitzroy Dearborn Publishers, 1998.

Spector, Amy. "Ed LaDou: The 'Prince' of Pizza Finds a New Loyal Following." *Nation's Restaurant News,* March 15, 1999.

Station.com, "EverQuest II - /pizza". *Station.com,* April 28, 2005, https://web.archive.org/web/20050428085144/http:/everquest2.station.sony.com/pizza/.

Stewart, Jocelyn Y. "Ed LaDou, 52; Chef Pioneered Gourmet Pizza Revolution." *Los Angeles Times,* January 4, 2008.

Straus, Karen Cope. "Alice Waters: Earth Mother of California Cuisine." *Vegetarian Times,* June 1997.

The Consortium for the Protection of the Mozzarella di Bufala Campana website, About Us https://www.mozzarelladop.it/en/consortium/.

Toledo, Sérgio. "São Paulo Consome Mais Pizza do que a Itália." *Jornal do Brasil,* August 27, 2007, https://www.jb.com.br/economia/noticias/2007/08/27/sao-paulo-consome-mais-pizza-do-que-a-italia.html.

Uebelherr, Jan. "Joseph Simek was a founder of Tombstone Pizza." *Milwaukee Journal Sentinel,* February 20, 2013, https://archive.jsonline.com/news/obituaries/simek-a-founder-of-tombstone-pizza-has-died-g08rrao-192103331.html/.

Vaccaro, Chris R. "Joe's Pizza Honors Giants with Blue Pie." *Patch.com,* Jan 24, 2012, https://patch.com/new-york/sachem/joe-s-pizza-honors-giants-with-blue-pie.

Wahlberg, Maria. "Svenska dagbladet: Pizza Statistics According to AC Nielsen." *SvD.se,*

January 13, 2005, https://www.svd.se/norrmannen-varldsbast-pa-att-ata-pizza.

Wiener, Scott. "A Brief History of the Pizza Slicer." *Serious Eats. Scott's Pizza Chronicles*, December 8, 2012.

Wilcox, Mike. "Tasters Disagree Pizza Test Proves No One is Best." *The Reminder*, September 27, 1979.

Wohleber, Curt. "Frozen Pizza." *American Heritage's Invention & Technology*, Winter 2005, Issue 3.

Wolfson, Andrew. "The Real Papa John: Pizza Entrepreneur John Schnatter Makes No Apologies for Wealth, Success, Obamacare Remarks | Math Whiz Mixed Pizza Passion, Finance." *The Courier-Journal*, January 13, 2013.

Zdechlich, Mark. "The Economic War Among the States: The Pizza King and the Perils of Bidding." (transcript), *Minnesota Public Radio*, April 9, 1996.

Index